REFRAMING CAREER SUCCESS

Picture Your Significance at Work
from a Christian Perspective

Kevin Anselmo

Words of praise about this book from some notable names as well as unheralded professionals who personify success from a Christian perspective.

"The principles highlighted in *Reframing Career Success* align to our basketball program's goal to develop champions for life in which character and spiritual development are paramount. The book will help you define what true career success entails with eternal perspective." —**Scott Drew**, head coach of the 2021 Baylor Men's Basketball NCAA Championship Team and author of *The Road to J.O.Y.*

"Healing words for a professional world scarred by self-idolatry." —**Mark Schaefer**, author of *Marketing Rebellion*

"Mother Teresa once noted that we are called to be faithful, not successful from an earthly perspective. With that in mind, I am grateful for this practical approach on how to define and action true success at work from a Christian point of view." —**Bethany Anderson**, missionary and founder of the Hope Adventure

"What does success at work mean, and how does it connect with our faith journey? In his book, Kevin Anselmo helps us answer these questions from multiple perspectives. Connecting the heart, mind and spirit, this book will enable you to create your own career success definition and related metrics that will guide your actions and decisions at work." —**Sanyin Siang**, author of *The Launch Book* and CEO Coach

"Whether your career has had the success you desired or come up shorter than you'd hoped, this book will help you reflect on your career journey and find the significance we all want from our work." —**David Burkus**, author of *Leading from Anywhere*

"Teachers sometimes never see the impact of our efforts, and discouragement can diminish our original enthusiasm. Reframing Career Success helped me to think deeply about my career goals and to clearly define what career success means to me as a Christ follower and a teacher. It is an important read for teachers and other professions." —**Jessica Stock**, teacher Sarasota County

"Read this book if you're struggling to understand the significance of your work. It will help you reframe what success on the job means from the only point of view that really matters." —**Mope Ogunsulire**, partner at Sahel Capital

"This book is an important guide for understanding how the gospel message can provide everlasting peace throughout the highs and lows of our career journeys. Learning not to separate your faith from your work is such an incredible gospel-centric idea that is reinforced throughout the pages of this book. Recommended both for ambitious professionals in the marketplace and pastors looking for faith and career content to support their congregations." —**Dr. Nic Williams**, lead pastor at South Shore Community Church and author of *When Fear and Faith Collide*

<u>Free Download</u>

Define Your Career Success Worksheet

Download a free "Career Success Definition" worksheet. Type in your response, drawing inspiration from the principles covered in this book. Then save the worksheet to your desktop or print out the document and put it in a visible place as a reminder of your definition. Sign up at www.reframingcareersuccess.com.

Table of Contents

Introduction

Imagine in front of you, right now, there is an empty picture frame hanging on the wall. There is no image within this frame—yet.

Envision that this frame will highlight your ideas of career success. What words and pictures would you put inside this frame? Which metrics would you include? Are you only incorporating performance-oriented results? Have you considered a Christian perspective?

We all subconsciously work with an image of success in our minds. But most haven't processed what career success actually entails. So, this image is not clear. It is jumbled and pixelated. Or it is littered with too many elements. The picture within the frame is either empty, skewed or incomplete.

We are bombarded by stories of people who achieve great fame and fortune. They are often considered heroes and the barometers of success. The standards of others—not necessarily aligned to our values—subconsciously creep into our thinking and actions.

This fuzzy picture impacts how we work. It can cause us to question our identity when we don't reach our goals. Are we failures? What is the significance of our work? Some people attribute success to "God's blessing." Does that mean those who fail are not enjoying the favor of God? When faced with a career disappointment, should we persevere, like so many famous business heroes, or do we need to pivot?

These are the types of questions I have wrestled with for some time as a result of some of my own personal experiences. I know that I am not alone.

- At a large multinational company, there is only one CEO, yet there are hundreds of employees at various levels of management who have never fulfilled a dream of being the chief decision-maker.
- For every entrepreneur making seven figures per year and now sitting out on the beach drinking tequilas all day, there are thousands of business owners who are working very hard, frustrated that their one big idea hasn't caught on yet.
- For every musician who has created a top hit, there are thousands who wonder why they can't experience a similar destiny as they perform in coffee shops and bars in front of small crowds.
- There are countless people whose career aspirations have been derailed due to various circumstances beyond their control: an abusive or narcissistic boss, unfair politics and personal tragedies to name a few.
- Others have long desired to create an impact in their jobs, but for whatever reason have become stagnant and disenchanted with their work.
- Some have achieved big goals but still feel dissatisfaction. Maybe it is the pressure to replicate results. Or perhaps it is realizing that the glory of achievement is soon forgotten. For whatever reason, there is discontentment despite the accomplishments.

If you can relate to any of these examples, this book is for you. This book is also for me. In an introduction, we often read about all the accolades of the author to establish this person's credibility. In this case, part of the author's bio is not about rosy accomplishments but rather disappointments and a quest to understand success.

Since 2013, I have been running my own communications consulting company, Experiential Communications. Over the years, there have been different ups and downs. I have been hard on myself when ideas haven't caught on.

For example, in 2019, I came up with what I thought was a brilliant idea: Global Innovators Academy. I am passionate about teaching digital communications skills. One day, while driving to a client engagement and listening to an audiobook on innovation in education, I thought my big entrepreneurial light-bulb moment had arrived. I needed to start an educational program that enabled high school and college students to interview innovators and then write articles to be published online. The individuals to be interviewed would align to the students' career aspirations. It would be a win-win-win for the student, the person being interviewed and the sponsoring institution.

In my mind, I thought this could be the next major innovation in education. Just as Khan Academy has transformed how students learn about math through fun and informative online learning experiences, Global Innovators Academy could have a significant impact in enabling students to learn important communications skills in the process of interviewing interesting people.

I set out to make this vision a reality and put together a great curriculum. I invested in professional video educational content and hired a coach to guide me along in the process. Then I began marketing the program in 2020. I knocked on many doors. Pounded the pavement. Wrote articles. Did podcast interviews. Created social media content.

The response from the market wasn't what I had envisioned. I was able to identify a few partners. The overwhelming number of students who went through the program seemed to genuinely enjoy it. However, as of this writing, it doesn't seem like this program will be the "Khan Academy" of digital communications. In fact, it seems like it will only account for a small percentage of my annual income.

Throughout this journey, I questioned my own abilities. My idea seemed noble. As a practicing Christian, my intent was to use this initiative for God's glory in different ways. Why would God not answer my career-related prayers? Why was this initiative not successful the way I envisioned it? Why did I feel that my efforts were insignificant? Perhaps you have similar stories and can relate to these reactions.

Over the past year or so, I have spent countless hours thinking about professional success and disappointments through the lens of the Christian faith. I have spoken with many people about different topics around faith and work journeys. My quest to answer some of my own questions has sent me down a path to countless related Google searches, books, an exploration through the Bible and deep personal reflection. In the process, I identified 12 important principles to help you capture a complete image of what significance at work entails from a Christian perspective.

I am not a very good photographer. My wife Nicole jokingly reminds me of this almost every time I take a picture of her with our two children. Nevertheless, I admire quality photography and chose to use the metaphor of taking a picture throughout this book. A photographer uses various techniques to capture a moment in time. We can apply some of a photographer's process to capture a definition and the meaning of career success for ourselves.

To begin, we first need to zoom out and consider the reality of our environment, so Part 1 includes the following principles:

- **Principle #1:** God Is in Control
- **Principle #2:** The Captain of Your Career (Hint: It's Not You!)
- **Principle #3:** The Cost of Success
- **Principle #4:** The Cross

Photographers need to avoid certain angles. Raising or lowering the camera an inch can be the difference between a great and terrible picture, depending on the location of the subject. In creating your picture of career success, you need to be aware of two different angles that can cause distortion:

- **Principle #5:** Career Idealism
- **Principle #6:** Workplace Idols

For Part 3, we will zoom in to examine the details of your career success picture:

- **Principle #7:** Define Your Career Success
- **Principle #8:** Write Out Your Metrics

To make a great shot even better, a photographer fine-tunes an image with various post-production editing techniques. For the purpose of this book, the fine-tuning of your career success picture involves the final four principles in Part 4:

- **Principle #9:** Stop Comparing
- **Principle #10:** Express Gratitude
- **Principle #11:** Pray with Perspective
- **Principle #12:** Discover Growth and New Direction

This framing can provide us with a sense of everlasting peace and motivation that transforms how we work. Therefore, it's optimal that your career success picture is visible in some way. So, after covering these principles, the conclusion of this book provides tips for creating a tangible picture that you will see regularly. This reminder of your career success definition can guide how you work.

Your career success picture will be informed in part by the questions that are highlighted at the end of each chapter. Warning: these are very difficult questions. I certainly don't have the answers to these questions all figured out. Many are questions that we should be grappling with for the rest of our lives. For this and other reasons, I highly recommend that you attempt to answer some of these questions with a friend, colleague or mentor. They would also be ideal to discuss as part of a small group or class.

For most of the 12 principles, you will read about related stories and examples. Where applicable, I highlight research from different academic publications as well as career and workplace best practices coming from blogs, podcasts, books and articles in mainstream media.

Each chapter includes references and examples from the Bible that relate to the principle in some way. I know many like to pluck verses from the Bible to selfishly support whatever claim they are trying to make. Terrible dictators and political leaders have used scripture to support violating others' rights. Cognizant of this, I have done my best to be as thorough as possible to ensure that I am not using such sacred text in any inappropriate manner. I am not a philosopher or theologian, so I am grateful to those much wiser and theologically sound than I who have shared their feedback.

Note that there are some ways in which God makes his intentions known to us. There are many more areas where we as humans can't understand. I want to be most respectful in interpreting Christian principles where applicable while not overstepping my place in declaring our heavenly *Father's* will as a *child* of God. In my writing, you will see that some absolutes are communicated with certainty. You will often see language around "I would think" or "I believe" as my belief and understanding could be open to different interpretations.

Note that these principles are subjective. If anyone else were to write this book, they might come up with a completely different list of the 12 most important Christian principles for defining career success and putting our workplace disappointments into proper context. I believe that these principles reflect the Christian message, but they aren't literally "the gospel." For that, see Matthew, Mark, Luke and John of the Holy Bible instead.

I have shared who this book is for and what it is about. It is important to clarify what this book isn't about. Please don't read this book to find:

- Quick and easy goal execution tactics so you can "live the life you always imagined."
- Best practices on how to go from "rags to riches."
- Prayer techniques to deploy so that God will abundantly provide you with lots of money, possessions and career recognition.

This book is the antithesis to these types of so-called promises that you can easily find in your local bookstore, perusing on Amazon and as Facebook sponsored content. Go elsewhere if you are looking for such perspectives. If, however, you need honest and pragmatic ideas on how to be at peace and motivated throughout the highs and lows of your career journey, then the content in this book is for you.

A quick message to anyone checking this out who doesn't adhere to or is skeptical of the Christian faith. Perhaps you are appalled by the politicization of the "evangelical" movement, disgusted by stories of preachers who have abused their power or nauseated by prosperity gospel teachings. Maybe the church in some way has let you down, and you find it bizarre how people misuse ancient religious texts. I understand, but please don't leave. I particularly invite you to explore the content here. I don't want to "impose" my own Christian faith on you, but I do aim to provide you encouragement and, hopefully, new perspectives.

The average person spends some 90,000 hours at work over the course of a lifetime.[1] That is approximately one third of our lives. So many of us trudge through those 90,000 hours and go through the motions as part of our routines. Many toil away in frustration due to a host of different unmet goals and professional letdowns.

Writing this book has been the most important project of my career so far. Thinking deeply about how faith and career connect has completely changed my approach to work. Extracting what true success entails from a Christian perspective has been liberating. I believe—and pray—that the same can happen for you in reading this book.

We can't afford to waste these 90,000 lifetime work hours plagued by discontentment and frustration. Let's make sure to spend these hours optimally! On that note, let's dive in and begin creating your career success picture.

PART I

ZOOMING OUT
ON THE REALITIES
OF OUR ENVIRONMENT

Principle #1: God Is in Control

Let's assume that you invest in real estate—we'll say buildings. You put a significant amount of your net worth into an investment. Then, a short time later, the investment literally burns to the ground. Following this, just two years later, you face the hardship of losing several loved ones in a travel-related accident.

What would you do? Would you proclaim, "It is well with my soul"?

Meet someone who did this: Horatio Spafford. A senior partner of a large law firm, Horatio lost a significant financial investment during the Great Fire of Chicago in 1871. Then in 1873, his four daughters were killed as their ship set sail from the United States to England. Horatio learned about the death of his daughters via a telegram from his wife Anna, who survived the shipwreck. As he sailed to Europe from the United States to meet with his wife, he penned the hymn "It Is Well with My Soul." I think these are some of most beautiful words ever put to song:

> When peace, like a river, attendeth my way,
> When sorrows like sea billows roll,
> Whatever my lot, Thou has taught me to say,
> It is well, it is well with my soul.[2]

How is a person able to write this after such a tragedy? I was hoping to find some remnant from Horatio's life in which he explained how he had been able to respond to such a major career disappointment exacerbated by personal tragedy. No such interview exists. After all, it was some 150 years ago when this happened. There is no Horatio Spafford blog or YouTube channel. Perhaps the hymn tells us everything we need to know about his mindset. The words he put to song following a terrible tragedy underscore one key point: God is in control.

The Chicago fire killed approximately 300 people, destroyed roughly 3.3 square miles of the city, including over 17,000 structures, and left more than 100,000 residents homeless. The fire is claimed to have started in or around a small barn belonging to the O'Leary family. The initial response by the fire department was quick, but due to an error by the watchman, Matthias Schaffer, the firefighters were sent to the wrong place, allowing the fire to grow unchecked.[3]

Horatio could have vented anger at these perpetrators of the fire. He could have been plagued by jealousy as he looked at other buildings in Chicago that were unscathed by the fire. After all, the owners of those buildings were able to grow their investments. He could have assumed that the Lord was punishing him. He could have worked tirelessly to recuperate his lost wealth.

Obviously, something went terribly wrong for a ship to wreck. Horatio could have harbored resentment towards the captains, crew and others involved in the accident.

There must have been times of intense grieving and questioning God. That would only be a natural human reaction. But, as we see from the lyrics of "It Is Well with My Soul," Horatio was somehow able to zoom out and see that God was in control in the midst of horrible circumstances.

Towards the end of their lives, Anna and Horatio resettled in Jerusalem. They formed a society that engaged in philanthropic work amongst the people of Jerusalem, regardless of religious affiliation.

Lessons from Job on How to Deal with Terrible Circumstances

There are a number of ways that control and disappointment play out in the Bible, including the story of Job. Here is a man who we know was very successful. Job had great wealth and a terrific family. Job 1:3 states that "He was the greatest man among all people of the East." One can assume that he had great career success to generate such a standing.

Then one day that was all taken away from him. He experienced a series of terrible tragedies, including the loss of all his possessions and the deaths of his children. The book of Job details the mourning and anguish that he experienced. He utters the following in Job 1:20–21: "Naked I came from my mother's womb, and naked I will depart. The Lord gave, and the Lord has taken away; may the name of the Lord be praised."

For many chapters in the book of Job, we get a glimpse into his conversations with friends about his plight. These interactions might be like the ones we'd have with a friend, colleague or spiritual advisor following a setback. The friends seem to have a black and white view of the world and equate Job's misfortune to a curse from God. Despite being angry and confused, Job doesn't agree with their assessment.

Interestingly, God speaks to Job through a storm and engages in a lively dialogue. In Job 38:4–7, God asks him, "Where were you when I laid the earth's foundation? Tell me, if you understand. Who marked off its dimensions? Surely you know! Who stretched a measuring line across it? On what were its footings set, or who laid its cornerstone—while the morning stars sang together and all the angels shouted for joy?"

Over the next chapter and a half, God asks Job some 45 different rhetorical questions of this nature. In essence, God is telling Job who is boss and that he is in control. We see Job's response in chapter 42:2–3: "I know that you can do all things; no purpose of yours can be thwarted. You asked, 'Who is this that obscures my plans without knowledge?' Surely I spoke of things I did not understand, things too wonderful for me to know."

Interestingly, God doesn't actually provide Job direct rationale of why he experienced such terrible suffering. However, the reader of Job actually catches a glimpse of this question in the first chapter. We read of an encounter between Satan and God. Satan opines that Job would turn away from God if his fortune were taken away. God then gives Satan permission to cause calamity in Job's personal life.

It can be hard for us as human beings to understand why God allowed this. See the list of 45+ questions that God asked Job beginning in chapter 38 for a greater perspective. We do learn that Job never lost his belief in God despite being confused and upset by his circumstances.

Ultimately, his fortunes were restored. This is not prescriptive. We shouldn't necessarily expect the same result by mimicking Job's response in a 21st-century setting. Rather, this response by Job illustrates the power of submitting to a God who is in control and whose thinking and actions are beyond us.

A New Testament verse that also summarizes the power of an all-knowing and powerful God is I Corinthians 2:11: "For who knows a person's thoughts except their own spirit within them? In the same way no one knows the thoughts of God except the Spirit of God."

God's Sovereignty

I think we need to be careful about spending exorbitant amounts of time considering why God allows certain events to happen in our vocational pursuits. It can lead us to question how well God is doing his job.

There is a terrific scene from the movie *Rudy* that illustrates this point. The main character, Rudy, is despondent as his dream of playing football at the University of Notre Dame isn't going according to plan. Rudy wonders if he hasn't been praying fervently enough and asks Father John Cavanaugh if there is anything else that he can do. Father Cavanaugh responds, "Son, in 35 years of religious studies, I have come up with two hard, inconvertible facts. There is a God, and I am not him."[4]

Father Cavanaugh demonstrated that there is great conviction and truth to saying "I don't know." He is essentially deferring to God's sovereignty. Likewise, we don't always need to have an answer to why God is allowing us to experience some sort of career disappointment. The same also applies to our successes.

We want to control our lives as much as possible. When life becomes a whirlwind, we at least want to try controlling the narrative. Perhaps this causes us to question God.

Raj Raghunathan, a professor at the University of Texas McCombs School of Business and author of *If You're So Smart, Why Aren't You Happy*, writes about the deep-seated desire humans have for control and certainty. He

> Ultimately, we are under the control of a higher being. The quicker we can accept that, the better!

highlights research showing that control helps us to believe that we can shape outcomes and events to our liking.[5] It also gives us the sense that we are not under the control of others.

To some extent, it seems like a false hope. Sometimes, we are directly responsible for our career disappointments. Other setbacks are completely out of our control. We have hardly any influence on major events, such as pandemics, wars and famines.

In November 2019, nobody knew anything about COVID-19. Within months, it would upend our way of living and working. Fast forward a couple of years and it would be difficult to find anybody whose work hasn't been altered in some way due to the pandemic—an event beyond our control. Some have benefited positively; the majority haven't.

Ultimately, we are under the control of a higher being. The quicker we can accept that, the better!

The reality is that we all face career disappointments. We can choose to use our energy to store up resentment against the boss who didn't give us the promotion or the prospective client who rejected our brilliant idea. We can direct our ire to the policies of government officials whose actions are somehow related to our professional setback. We can question why a just God would allow hard-working and well-intended people to face trials.

While there are appropriate times for grieving a setback, harboring these types of feelings over the long-term will result in never-ending misery. If we are ever able to say and mean, "Whatever my lot, it is well with my soul," then we will surely be able to find peace and contentment in the midst of the setback and the motivation to make a difference in our calling.

You may find it admirable how Job and Horatio responded to trials. Perhaps you can see the merit of such an approach. But how does one live this out practically? I can't imagine how I would respond if I lost a significant amount of my life savings to some type of mishap and if that was coupled with some sort of family tragedy. I very much question if, after a grieving process, I could truly proclaim that "it is well with my soul" and dedicate my remaining years to the service of others.

My guess would be that adopting such an approach entails some universal principles that we can tailor and personalize based on our own personalities and strengths. For me, I am better equipped to deal with difficult career outcomes by focusing regularly on the truths of the Bible, taking part in volunteer activities, submitting to God's will regularly through prayer and meditation, and incorporating people in my network who appreciate spiritual impact over earthly accomplishments.

Personally, writing about these topics is very helpful in thinking about career goals and the spiritual dimension. There is something about writing that forces me to wrestle with different topics, gain clarity and attempt to communicate such ideas as coherently as possible. We are all different. Consider various approaches that work for you.

Zoom Out on the Realities of Your Environment

Here are some questions and points to consider (ideally to discuss with a friend or in a small group):

- What do you think contributed to Horatio Spafford and Job's responses to their devastating setbacks?

- How have you responded to career setbacks (either currently or in the past)? In what ways has your response been appropriate and healthy? In what ways has your response been detrimental?

- What practices should you adopt to best prepare yourself for career disappointments—large or small—that inevitably will come your way? (As you consider this question, I encourage you to listen to "It Is Well with My Soul." On YouTube, you can find either a classical rendition or a popular modern version sung by Kristene DiMarco).

Principle #2: The Captain of Your Career (Hint: It's Not You!)

The 2009 film *Invictus* is quite inspiring. It details the riveting story of how South Africa hosted and won the 1995 Rugby World Cup. It was the first major sporting event to take place in South Africa following the end of apartheid. Against difficult circumstances, South Africa won behind the support of President Nelson Mandela and a unified country.[6]

In one particularly powerful scene in the movie, Mandela, played by Morgan Freeman, meets with captain Francois Pienaar, played by Matt Damon. Mandela encourages Pienaar to lead his team to victory, citing the Invictus poem written by William Ernest Henley in 1875. This poem had inspired Mandela while he had been imprisoned on Robben Island for 18 years. The poem concludes as follows:

> It matters not how strait the gate,
> How charged with punishments the scroll,
> I am the master of my fate,
> I am the captain of my soul.[7]

As the film concludes, Morgan Freeman recites these last lines while raucous fans in the background celebrate an inspiring victory that had remarkable significance given the current events in South Africa. The scene can give a person goosebumps.

The philosophy of these last two lines in the poem—"I am the master of my fate, I am the captain of my soul"—is immersed into the conversation around careers. Popular themes are:

- Own your career.
- You are the CEO of you.

18

Principle #2: The Captain of Your Career
(Hint: It's Not You!)

- You are the master of your career.

In many ways, we do have more control over our careers than at any point in history, thanks in large part to technology and the internet. In decades past, the local newspaper's classified section and word of mouth were the main ways to be aware of career opportunities. It was arduous to fax or mail a résumé over to a potential employer.

Now we can apply for different jobs anywhere in the world with just a few clicks of the mouse. We can demonstrate credentials through our online activity and access educational content to grow in areas that support our career aspirations. Remote work and the gig economy have further opened opportunities that would have been completely implausible to a previous generation.

Also integrated into this mix is a world of social media. We can all go to the channel of our choice to see individuals highlight, for the most part, the most glamorous aspects of their careers. This can lead to a range of reactions. One of these may be that we should all be doing more to take control of our careers to enjoy work and life in the same way that XYZ person on social media so proclaims.

It is indeed true that we have the opportunity to be more thoughtful about our work possibilities, thus aligning to the notion of being the captain of our fate and soul.

The problem is that we have gone too far in sharing a message to a generation of workers that the personal actions we take in our careers, that we control, will lead to happiness and contentment. It has backfired. The "own your career and be happy" message is not working.

In 2021, more people left their work voluntarily than at any point in history. Experts and scholars will be researching for years the causes and impact of this Great Resignation. It seems that many people reconsidered their lives and what is important in the midst of the pandemic. Many of the people resigning from their jobs felt disconnected. Employee morale is increasingly on the decline, as evidenced by work engagement scores.[8]

There are unintended letdowns that are not communicated in the "you are the master of your career and happiness" message.

It is nice to think that the outcomes of our work are 100 percent the result of our abilities and the hard work we have poured into our crafts. Unfortunately, that often isn't the case. There are so many ways this is evident.

It starts at birth, the epitome of a circumstance that is beyond our control. About 15 percent of people live in developed countries. The rest live in developing and undeveloped countries. There are tremendous disparities in wealth (or lack thereof). If you were born in a richer country, you—by default—have set yourself up for far greater career success if income is the key metric.

There are surely hundreds of circumstances beyond our control that have influenced our career journeys. Looking back, I can see countless ways situations completely beyond my control influenced my career, both positively and negatively. If you do the same, you will see this to be the case as well.

Alex Trebek, in his memoir *The Answer Is . . .: Reflections on My Life*, shared the key to how he became the host of

Jeopardy, the quiz show watched by millions. For Alex, it came down to one word—Luck! He wrote:

> My broadcasting experience wouldn't have mattered much if they hadn't been producing game shows at the time—if Westerns or reality television or Judge Judy-type courtrooms had been in vogue. Yes, hard work and experience are essential. But so is timing. And luck. Don't ever discount the importance of luck in terms of determining your opportunities and your future.[9]

He goes on to detail in the book how a series of random events led to his becoming the host of the popular show.

God's timing is often different than the timing we have in mind. Illustrating how the impact of our work is beyond our control, consider the example of many authors whose books gained significant traction after they had died. Google the phrase "authors who became famous after they died," and you will see a plethora of interesting examples. Among them is the American poet, Emily Dickinson. "Although Dickinson's acquaintances were most likely aware of her writing, it was not until after her death in 1886—when Lavinia, Dickinson's younger sister, discovered her cache of poems—that her work became public."[10]

Submitting to God as Our Career Captain

I think the notion of "I own my career" is perilous. But I don't believe that we should do the opposite and not take action based on the assumption that life is a random series of events. There is a better, more realistic approach that sits somewhere in the middle of those two philosophies. From a Christian perspective, I think it should go something like this:

- From "own your career" to "co-own your career" (and you have minority ownership).
- From being the "CEO of your career" to "being the CEO of your career, reporting to an almighty and powerful board." (Contrary to a CEO who reports to the board of directors on a quarterly basis, with this analogy, the chief decision-maker should consult with the board on an ongoing, continual basis).
- From "you are the master of your career" to "you are the faithful servant to the ultimate master."

Obviously, with these analogies, the majority owner, powerful board and ultimate master is God. A co-owner with minority ownership, the CEO reporting to the powerful board and the faithful servant all need to work hard and give their best effort. There are numerous benefits to both knowing and acting upon this hierarchy of God as the ultimate master of our career development.

It gives us the opportunity to reconsider the idea of control. For me, it is comforting to know that God controls every aspect of society and our personal lives. It provides perspective. We can work giving our best efforts, knowing that a higher being is really running the show. We can work to the best of our abilities, trusting that God has a reason for the unexpected circumstances that we might not be able to understand as humans.

God is the owner of our careers. We can accept that hierarchy or not. When we do so, it can help us to have a holistic approach to our career decision-making, both large and small.

PRINCIPLE #2: THE CAPTAIN OF YOUR CAREER
(HINT: IT'S NOT YOU!)

As an example of a big decision, let's say there is a person considering a job offer. The role is right up this person's alley. It is with a prestigious company that pays very well and offers terrific benefits. It would look great on a résumé and will be an interesting job to talk about at different social settings. However, the person has learned about some inappropriate behavior that takes place at this organization. It also seems that management has repeatedly ignored the transgressions.

A person whose identity is solely consumed by status will probably weigh the pros and cons quite differently than a person who reports to the powerful board of the Lord and, thus, factors in a set of variables that is focused on advancing the work of the Kingdom of God. At least that should be the case!

It can also impact smaller day-to-day decisions, such as finding the tone to use in an email to a colleague, taking credit ourselves or praising others for an achievement, using our time each day and navigating countless other scenarios.

With God as the all-powerful board of our career, we can reconsider our work successes and failures through a comprehensive set of metrics that is probably far more encompassing than what we might establish if left to our own devices. Those metrics will probably look different for each of us—see Part 3 for more on this topic.

God as Our Career Captain and the Bible

The notion of God as the captain of our careers is expressed both in the Old and New Testaments of the Bible. At the outset of the Bible, one of God's first commands is that we are to labor for six days and then rest on the seventh day.

> It is no coincidence that Jesus spent time in an ordinary profession just like most all of us.

In Genesis 2:15 we read: "Then the Lord God took the man and put him into the Garden of Eden to cultivate it and to keep it." Most all of us can appreciate the amount of work and effort that goes into keeping our homes and properties maintained, clean and orderly. Adam and Eve were given the task by God to cultivate and keep the Garden of Eden. While we are not provided specific measurements of this space, we can presume that cultivating and keeping this garden would require responsible and thoughtful work.

The book of Proverbs is filled with rich insights on why excellent work is important. I personally appreciate the following two verses:

> Proverbs 21:25—"The desire of the sluggard kills him, for his hands refuse to labor."
> Proverbs 12:14—"From the fruit of their lips people are filled with good things, and the work of their hands brings them reward."

Jesus, the Son of God, came down to earth and spent his young adult years as a carpenter before going into public ministry. Dr. Klaus Issler, professor at the Talbot School of Theology, notes that Jesus labored with his hands for about 20

24

years, six times as long as his three-year public ministry.[11] People even referred to Jesus by his profession as noted in Mark 6:3: "Isn't this the carpenter?" To me, associating an individual with their job usually signals a reputation for good work.

I would also think that it is no coincidence that Jesus spent time in an ordinary profession just like most all of us. Surely, as the Son of God, he could have just come down to earth, done some miracles, proclaimed that he was the chosen one, died on the cross and resurrected without toiling in a career. Perhaps God wants us to see that doing good work is so important that even Jesus would do this during his brief time on earth.

Practical Examples

Miguel Caraballo runs Limitless Investigations Solutions, an investigations company based in Sarasota, Florida. While he is the founder and runs the company primarily as a solo entrepreneur, his title is "managing member." This is deliberate, as Miguel is quick to point out that Jesus is the owner of the company.

"This is God's business, not my business," he said. "I report to God. More than anything, I want my work to help advance the kingdom of heaven on earth."

This impacts various aspects of his business. One that I found most interesting is that Miguel will dedicate specific days to pray for different clients.

When God is captain, it also helps us to deal with unmet goals. David Brühlmann, an author and consultant, said, "The key is to accept God's will and to seek first his kingdom. It is not a popular message in the 21st century, as we want it to be our way. But it's not about me. It is about putting God first and seeking his glory."

"Knowing that God is in control and working in me is not an excuse for laziness but a reason to work hard," added Martin Slack, pastor of Westlake Church in Switzerland. "It is about being diligent in the tasks he has given me. He is the boss, I am the undershepherd."

I can't promise that it is easy to adopt this approach of accepting that God is ultimately in charge of our careers. This applies for individuals working in the corporate world, entrepreneurs and even those involved with Christian ministry. We instinctively want to be in charge and also take actions that align solely to our individual self-interests.

But I do think that accepting this hierarchy brings far greater peace and motivation than relying just on our human powers. People who haven't reached their career goals can still review their character and take satisfaction as they seek to represent Christ to those around them, love their neighbor, pursue the common good, encourage others and diligently pursue their craft. God wants us to be good stewards of our talents. These differ for each person, but one constant is that we should do our best with the gifts and skills given to us.

It can be very freeing to connect your work to your faith. For one thing, it puts failures into perspective. Think about your most significant career disappointments. Do they still gnaw at you? We are, indeed, our greatest critics. Any embarrassing career setback is probably forgotten by others in a very short time. That is, unless you did something unethical that landed you in jail!

I recall an instance when I made an editing error, and an egregious mistake was sent out in a public newsletter. I was humiliated. I haven't forgotten about it some 20 years later. Nobody else remembers it today. Nobody else will be thinking about that mistake in the years to come. I doubt that, when the eulogy at my funeral is delivered, this professional hiccup will be highlighted! The same is true for your failures.

I also think that there is a connection between failures being forgotten and producing great work. For me, I do my best when I am not crippled by fear.

Take an athlete for example. When the coach is smothering—constantly yelling and barking orders—the athlete will usually not perform optimally. However, if the coach provides structure yet also provides the freedom to make a mistake, the athlete will usually play better.

This was true for me when I played amateur sports. In my professional career as a corporate communications professional and entrepreneur, I have worked both for people who have been more domineering and those who trusted me and saw mistakes as opportunities for learning. The latter has always been a more optimal experience. Perhaps the same is true for you as well.

Zoom Out on the Realities of Your Environment

Here are some questions and points to consider (ideally to discuss with a friend or in a small group).

- What is God's role in your career? Does he have a strong enough standing within the hierarchy?

- Think back to a difficult career situation. Did you consider the role of God as captain of your career in the midst of that predicament? If yes, how did this give you peace? If not, how do you think you would have reacted differently?

- What are practical ways to incorporate God as the ultimate CEO in your career journey?

Principle #3: The Cost of Success

For every best-selling author, there are probably thousands of writers who wish they could claim the title. In reality, their work is read by a very small audience. For every famous celebrity, there are many people who long to have some sort of public glory, but their good work goes unrecognized instead. You can apply this same logic for many other professions and scenarios.

Consider that, maybe, those thousands of people who haven't fulfilled that burning desire for top achievement are better off. As you zoom out on the realities of your environment, perhaps the same is true for you. Here are some possible reasons that could be the case. (Please note that if you are the best-selling author, CEO or award-winning singer, I extend my congratulations! The below "maybes" don't necessarily mean that I am describing you.)

Success Could Go to Your Head

"Don't let failure go to your heart, and don't let success go to your head."[12] This was advice shared to Will Smith by his grandmother. I guess he didn't heed these words when he decided to slap Chris Rock at the Oscars Awards Ceremony! Nevertheless, perhaps your grandmother or a mentor once shared similar words of wisdom with you.

The quarterly peer-reviewed scientific journal *Human Performance* defines arrogance as "stable belief of superiority and exaggerated self-importance that are manifested with excessive and presumptuous claims."[13] I don't know many who would be proud to associate with such a definition. Yet, doesn't it seem that many leaders in the highest positions of organizations reek of arrogance and bravado?

There are exceptions, of course. I love what NBA superstar Giannis Antetokounmpo said at a press conference when asked how he appears to not have a big ego. He said, "When I think about, 'Oh, I did this,' or, 'I'm so great,' usually the next day you're going to suck. The next few days, you're going to be terrible." He then added, "When you focus on the past, that's your ego. When I focus on the future, that's my pride. I try to focus in the moment, in the present. That's humility."[14]

For many, it is difficult to have this approach when reaching the top of their profession. Note that mentors never needed to advise others about how failure or lack of goal achievement can lead to arrogance. But when reaching the mountaintop, we need to be particularly wary of letting our achievements distort our perceptions of ourselves.

You Still Might Not Be Satisfied

Netflix's documentary, *The Last Dance*, captures the mindset of basketball star Michael Jordan and his obsession to continually excel. In one way, it is commendable to see an athlete, or any professional for that matter, strive for excellence.

However, there were times Jordan crossed the line in his quest to remain at the top. The film shows poignant scenes of Jordan belittling teammates. Decades later, when interviewed for *The Last Dance*, Jordan seemed to struggle to justify some of his actions. In one scene, he tried excusing his behavior and teared up. He abruptly stopped and requested the camera crew to break.[15]

The high of success is also short-lived. Jordan's coach, Phil Jackson, summarized this following the Bulls' second title when he said, "You're only a success for the moment that you complete a successful act."[16]

I can imagine that this lack of contentment, even when reaching the top, can play out in a number of other career journeys, such as the following:

> The high of success is short-lived.

- A professor who ultimately accomplishes the goal of becoming dean will constantly be looking over her shoulder to make sure that nobody else is trying to take that role.
- An entrepreneur who has cracked the top 100 wealthiest individuals in the world will not be satisfied until he becomes number one. If that goal were to be achieved, then staying in that spot would be paramount.
- A once-starving artist who becomes nationally recognized won't be content until she wins the top award for the category.

Curtis Jackson, also known as the rapper 50 Cent, confessed in his book *Hustle Harder* that even though he has been comfortable sharing his successes publicly, privately he has been sensitive to the fact that those accomplishments have led to mistakes with money, relationships, opportunities and friendships.[17]

While definitely less glamorous, I can also attest to how obtaining my goals hasn't brought complete satisfaction. Throughout my 20 years of professional experience, I have both fallen short on some goals and secured some achievements. In high school, I recall telling an adult that my goal was to work in sports communications. This gentleman told me that I would be wasting my time and that breaking into this field was unattainable. However, I was able to achieve this goal and had the opportunity to work for two international sport federations based in Europe. I covered international baseball and basketball competitions around the world, including the 2000 Sydney Olympic Games.

Yet, even when I fulfilled this goal, I wasn't content. I still longed for further significance. I became disheartened when I realized that workplace politics and mundane tasks were part of working in the sports communications field (at least in my case).

The same can be said for when I started my own communications consulting company back in 2013. I have been extremely fortunate to run my own business from the comfort of the lanai in my backyard in Sarasota, Florida, working on (mostly) interesting projects with clients from around the world while financially supporting my family in the process. If you had told me that this would be a reality in 2010, I would have been thrilled. While I am grateful for this reality, I have realized that this achievement doesn't bring complete and total fulfillment.

No matter how much we achieve, we will always be looking for more. To a certain extent, the nonstop pursuit of our ambitious goals is like feeding an insatiable appetite.

There is actually a scientific concept that vividly illustrates this called the "hedonic treadmill." When human beings experience something good—such as securing a terrific job promotion—the surge of happiness that's experienced is likely to return to a steady personal baseline over time. The hedonic treadmill also applies to difficult events. When people experience a loss or setback, the feelings that accompany the negative event lessen in severity over time.[18]

While not rooted in any faith-based context, the hedonic treadmill aligns to the Christian principle that we should not be looking for life events to provide satisfaction. The hedonic treadmill runs counter to hedonism—the notion that pleasure should be the aim of human behavior.

As you grapple with different career highs and lows, please keep this in mind. Even if you did achieve that gold standard you have set your eyes upon, you still wouldn't have total peace and contentment once you achieved that goal. Such peace can only come from a higher being!

You Could Lose Perspective

One morning, I was having coffee with my friend Jonathan Fleming, a talented musician living in Sarasota, Florida. We were discussing goals and career disappointments. While he aspires to create music that reaches masses, to date this hasn't happened. Rather, he plays at the church and in front of small crowds at bars and coffee shops.

"I don't know if I could ever handle the fame," he shared. "It could be a blessing in disguise that I never have hit it big."

Jonathan is essentially heeding the advice of Proverbs 29:23, which says, "Pride brings a person low..." You can serve God whether you are addressing the masses or a small number of individuals. It requires more discipline to keep the focus on bringing glory to God as our work is increasingly recognized by others.

Surely, many of you reading this book can point to a former friend or colleague who previously was down to earth and always available for a good chat. Then, after hitting a milestone, this person almost seems too important to interact with you.

Sadly, the pitfalls of success are evident even for those working in Christian ministry. To see this on display, check out the Christianity Today podcast *The Rise and Fall of Mars Hill.*[19] In great depth, it captures the story of how the Mars Hill Church's charismatic founder, Mark Driscoll, rose to fame through inspirational preaching that was listened to by millions on YouTube and iTunes. This was coupled with best-selling books read by many. As Driscoll became famous, he seemed to struggle with handling the celebrity culture that came with the fame. The podcast description notes, "The perils of power, conflict, and Christian celebrity eroded and eventually shipwrecked both the preacher and his multimillion-dollar platform." Driscoll is not the only such preacher who has fallen victim to those perils.

It is easy to point to people like Driscoll with disdain. While these individuals should be held to a higher standard as preachers of the Word of God, the reality is that we are all capable of losing perspective as we achieve big ambitious goals. There is probably only a minority of people on earth who are capable of achieving fame and glory yet remain grounded and humble (and in the case of Christians, maintaining their need for God).

Your Time Could Be Spent Differently

If you achieved your big goal, how would it affect your time? For many, the average day would look quite different.

In a *Harvard Business Review* article entitled "How CEOs manage time," Harvard Business School professors Michael E. Porter and Nitin Nohria wrote:

> CEOs are always on, and there is always more to be done. The leaders in our study worked 9.7 hours per weekday, on average. They also conducted business on 79% of weekend days, putting in an average of 3.9 hours daily, and on 70% of vacation days, averaging 2.4 hours daily. As these figures show, the CEO's job is relentless.[20]

These hours and demands probably look quite different from a middle manager's schedule.

A struggling writer who becomes a best-selling author might be traveling to give keynote talks around the world, meaning living on a plane and in hotels.

A lawyer at the firm in town might be working an average 40-hour work week. But, once elected to public office, this person suddenly needs to campaign around the clock to promote a particular agenda.

You can probably see a similar trend for many other professions in which the person reaches an ambitious goal. There is nothing wrong, per se, with work schedules evolving and changing. Some people are able to balance such work demands with other important priorities. But many can't.

In *The Financial Times* article titled "Good chiefs look after their family and spouse," venture capitalist Jon Moulton noted that CEOs are increasingly becoming more isolated due to the demands of the role.[21] This leads to a crisis of confidence that is ultimately detrimental to a leader's professional and personal life.

Think about the aspects of your life schedule that you value. Then remember that it could look quite different if you achieved a certain ambitious goal. Can this actually be a useful tradeoff?

You Could Lose Awareness of Your Need for God

Jesus said in Matthew 19:24 that "it is easier for a camel to go through the eye of a needle than for a rich man to enter into the kingdom of God." The saying was in response to a young rich man who had asked Jesus what was required to inherit eternal life.

Faith and finances are a delicate matter. There are many contrasting views. I am greatly offended by the surge of the "prosperity gospel"—the belief that God will provide material possessions and comforts to those who live a certain way. I hope to showcase this flawed theology throughout this book. At the other end of the spectrum, I don't believe that we should aspire to live in poverty. Being rich in itself is not necessarily wrong.

The metaphor of a camel going through the eye of a needle shared by Jesus is quite strong and rather hyperbolic. As opposed to being taken literally, I think it is probably meant to drive home this point: When we rely on our riches—whether accrued from career success or some other means—we are less aware of our need for God in our lives.

Pew Research underscores this point. It has continually shown a downward trend in the number of Christians in the United States. Christianity has also been on the decline in Europe for quite some time.[22] Meanwhile, Christianity is seeing increases in Africa and other parts of the majority world.[23]

There are a plethora of reasons for these trends. One of them has to do with the ways our success has eliminated our need to call upon a higher being to give us purpose, peace and daily bread.

Many followers of Christ have called upon God and been closest to him during the dark periods of life. If you aren't a Christian, perhaps you have similarly experienced the desire to pursue some sort of deeper quest for meaning and purpose when times have been bleaker in life. John Flavel, an English Puritan Presbyterian minister and author from the 1600s, argued in *Keeping the Heart* that the greatest spiritually dangerous situation to be in is prosperity. He wrote the following:

> When they were in a low condition, how humble, spiritual and heavenly they were but when advanced, what an apparent alteration has been upon their spirits! It was so with Israel; when they were in a low condition in the wilderness, then Israel was "holiness to the Lord:" but when they came into Canaan and were richly fed, their language was, "We are lords, we will come no more unto thee." Outward gains are ordinarily attended with inward losses.... [24]

Surely, there are people who can achieve the loftiest of their career aspirations and still see the need for God. But I would think it is much more difficult, as Jesus was probably trying to communicate in his exchange with the young wealthy man.

Disclaimer

As noted at the outset of this chapter, there are people who have reached the top of their professions and do stay grounded, are content, have perspective, spend their time wisely and call upon God daily for help and guidance.

Someone who appears to understand this, even at a very young age, is Scottie Scheffler. After winning the 2022 Masters golf tournament, he said:

> The reason why I play golf is I'm trying to glorify God and all that He's done in my life. So for me, my identity isn't a golf score. Like my wife Meredith told me this morning, "If you win this golf tournament today, if you lose this golf tournament by 10 shots, if you never win another golf tournament again, I'm still going to love you, you're still going to be the same person, Jesus loves you and nothing changes." All I'm trying to do is glorify God, and that's why I'm here. For me, it is not about a golf score.[25]

If you are like Scottie and have reached the top of your profession while maintaining such perspective, thank you for being such a positive example! It would be wise for all of us to pause and consider how we are best using our achievements for the betterment of others.

For every aspiring high achiever who hasn't reached the top of their mountain yet, this doesn't necessarily mean that you should abandon your big goals. Maybe we need to press on. In Principle 12, we will cover whether career disappointments mean that we should persevere or change course. I do think that it would be wise to question the driving forces inspiring you to achieve your big goals.

Zoom Out on the Realities of Your Environment

Here are some questions and points to consider (ideally to discuss with a friend or in a small group).

- What big unaccomplished goal do you wish to achieve? Why?

- How would achieving that goal impact your life? How would you view yourself differently? Would you view others differently? What would be your next goals? Would your values change?

- Are there pitfalls to success that you aren't realizing?

- How might achieving the big goal impact your relationship with God (both positively and negatively)?

Principle #4: The Cross

As we zoom out on our environment before honing in on our career success definition, let's consider Jesus Christ's work on earth. So many have experienced:

- Betrayal from a colleague or boss;
- Unjust blame for a situation and the negative consequences of workplace politics;
- Public humiliation, emotional trauma and abuse.

Meet someone who has experienced all these circumstances: Jesus of Nazareth, the Son of God.

Born some 2000+ years ago, Jesus entered the world as a King born to a peasant woman named Mary. After toiling in the everyday work of a carpenter, he lived out his public ministry for three and a half years, performing miracles, providing guidance to the masses and inviting people to follow him. From a human perspective, he then endured the most horrific of "career" disappointments ever known to man—death on the cross. However, this wasn't a disappointment for Jesus. In fact, it was the reason he came to the earth and is also a supreme example of how God is able to use a terrible event and transform it into something glorious.

We can certainly classify Christ's public ministry as his career—an individual's calling. We need to consider Jesus' life and how his death and resurrection can give us the ultimate peace and motivation in dealing with our career letdowns.

Workplace Betrayal

Workplace betrayals are terrible. Bosses take credit for work you did. Colleagues blame you for a problem that isn't your fault. The guilty colleagues know this to be the case, but they just want to cover their own butts. Then there is that good workplace friend who you later discover is slandering your name behind your back. There are a whole host of ways that betrayals happen on the job. These betrayals can be terrible to experience and can leave you feeling cynical and defeated.

> Take hope in that Jesus understands betrayal to the umpteenth degree.

Take hope in that there is a God out there who understands betrayal to the umpteenth degree. Jesus' two closest colleagues betrayed him in horrific ways. First, there is Jesus' best buddy at work, Peter. Think about the closest work colleague that you have ever had in your life. This is the person who you share meals with and spend countless hours talking through work and personal matters. That is like the relationship of Jesus and Peter.

Yet, at the most intense period of Jesus' public ministry— during his public arrest that would lead to his crucifixion— Peter ran miles away from Jesus. When a woman asked Peter if he was indeed a follower of Christ as she had assumed, Peter emphatically denied knowing him. This was just as Jesus had predicted.

Then, of course, there is the infamous Judas Iscariot, whose name is somewhat synonymous with the word "betrayal." Here is a person who was also one of Jesus' 12 chosen disciples. The betrayal he carries out is unlike anything you or I have experienced—the kind that ultimately leads to the victim's public and torturous death.

Blamed Unjustly

Have you ever been blamed for a workplace issue that wasn't your fault? Have workplace politics ever impacted you? If yes, you are not alone. Jesus was too.

He didn't do anything wrong. However, a group of people in high power across a certain influential group took umbrage at his proclamations, leading to a trial in front of a judicial body (the Sanhedrin) and then a public trial in front of the masses. The person with the ultimate power to free Jesus—Pontius Pilate—admitted to finding no fault, according to John 19:6. "As soon as the chief priests and their officials saw him, they shouted, 'Crucify! Crucify!' But Pilate answered, 'You take him and crucify him. As for me, I find no basis for a charge against him.'"

Imagine the injustice Jesus must have felt as the masses screamed to kill him and free Barabbas, described in the book of Matthew as a "notorious prisoner." Jesus is quiet and calm throughout the ordeal as he is tried for claiming to be the King of the Jews. Final verdict—guilty!

Public Humiliation and Emotional Trauma

Workplace trauma exists in many forms, including bullying, discrimination and various forms of harassment. The #MeToo movement has certainly shone a spotlight on the prevalence of sexual harassment in the workplace. The year 2020 was an incredibly tumultuous year that also put a spotlight on racial inequities in the workplace. Many people have been destroyed by the narcissistic behavior of bullying bosses and authorities.

Such actions have derailed the dreams of honest, hard-working employees.

Countless people have gone to workplace authorities to seek justice. The HR department sides with the person in power who is carrying out the abuse instead of believing the actual victim's version of events. Bosses manipulate the situation to save themselves, leaving innocent people distraught.

If you have ever been victimized in such an emotionally traumatic way, I am incredibly sorry. I can't imagine the pain that comes from not only the abuse itself but also the resulting disruption of possibly leaving a job and trying to find a different opportunity that provides some semblance of a safe working environment. There are many out there who are unable to leave their jobs for one reason or another and must somehow find the necessary strength to continue working in a dysfunctional environment. I can't comprehend how difficult this must be. If you were sitting next to me and telling me about such trauma, I would give you a hug and tell you I am sorry. Since we are not, I am giving an imaginary hug from afar.

I am not a psychologist and have no formal training in how to help those who have gone through these difficult circumstances. For this reason, I must confess that I feel ill-qualified to continue writing these next paragraphs.

With that disclaimer out of the way, I can share that there are ways the cross can serve as a source of peace and motivation to help us grapple with these types of awful circumstances.

God understands the deepest and saddest feelings stemming from abuse. Jesus was flogged in public. His clothes were torn off his body. After sharing the message that he was the Son of God for years, he died on a cross, naked for the world to see. His enemies put a crown of thorns on his head, mocking "the King of the Jews." Imagine the shame.

Like the victim at work going to the authorities to seek justice, so too did Jesus. As he was hanging on the cross, we read in Matthew 27:46: About three in the afternoon Jesus cried out in a loud voice, "Eli, Eli, lema sabachthani?" (which means, "My God, my God, why have you forsaken me?").

There was no answer. Moments later, Jesus was dead.

Peace and Motivation Through the Cross

We are human, and Jesus is God. He possessed the supernatural power to handle betrayals, injustices and public humiliation. He knew that it needed to be carried out as part of God's perfect plan. His resurrection was a supernatural event.

There are many ways in which we can't transfer our workplace disappointments to the story of Jesus' death and resurrection. However, there are some ways in which we can take the lessons from this most eventful moment in history and find peace and motivation as we deal with our workplace frustrations.

Understanding Our Pain

Jesus experienced pain as a human being in the most profound of ways. One of the beauties of the gospel message is that we have a God who became human.

On the career disappointment topic of harassment, I can't fully empathize with you, as I have never experienced this. But Jesus did. He wants us to call him and seek his help. He is

44

able to provide us comfort, as he experienced this problem first-hand and knows the way to overcome it.

Jesus' work on earth wasn't the dream life we are frequently sold in books and programs. There was no rags-to-riches story (at least in the literal sense). Actually, it was more like riches to rags. The apostle Paul highlights this in Philippians 2:5–8:

> In your relationships with one another, have the same mindset as Christ Jesus: Who, being in very nature God, did not consider equality with God something to be used to his own advantage; rather, he made himself nothing by taking the very nature of a servant, being made in human likeness. And being found in appearance as a man, he humbled himself by becoming obedient to death—even death on a cross!

Accepting God's Plan

Interestingly, Jesus didn't fight the betrayal and really didn't put up much resistance to those arresting him. He knew these events were coming and actually predicted it to all 12 of his disciples during the Last Supper. Jesus was deeply aware of God's purpose for his life on earth and also the fallen nature of the world.

I obviously don't think we should be sacrificial lambs in the workplace by allowing people to hurt us. We should certainly do everything within our power to stand up for justice. We should take the necessary action.

However, there will be times when our calls for justice go unanswered. As we rightfully grieve injustices, may we take solace that, in heaven, there is no abusive behavior and depravity. In the midst of such pain, may we take hope in the eternal realities that await us, just as Jesus did.

Forgiveness

This forgiveness flows to everyone—even to those same people who shouted, "Crucify him!" and put a crown of thorns on his head. Jesus was able to communicate directly with Peter, as is detailed in John 21. Forgiveness is granted, and we see that Jesus and Peter's relationship is restored. (Tragically, this didn't happen for Judas due to his suicide.)

Forgiving those who hurt us can be extremely difficult, especially if the perpetrators don't even offer an apology. Forgiveness doesn't excuse the harm done to you. But it does bring peace that helps us move on without bitterness and anger.

I know it is a whole lot easier to write about forgiveness as a helpful principle than it is to actually forgive, especially in cases of extreme exploitation. I would like to think that Jesus understands this too. Although different circumstances, it is noteworthy that the gospel message advanced only after forgiveness occurred.

Redemption

Not covered thus far in this chapter is how the crucifixion story plays out. We know that after Good Friday (Holy Friday), there is a victory at the end. Jesus experiences utter rejection and death itself before resurrecting after three days.

We see how this dramatic death and resurrection impacted a small group of individuals who risked their lives to spread the message of the power of Jesus Christ, sparking the greatest movement over the past 2,000 years. It is because of the death and resurrection of Jesus that the apostle Paul writes in Romans 5:3–5:

> Not only that, but we rejoice in our sufferings, knowing that suffering produces endurance, and endurance produces character, and character produces hope, and hope does not put us to shame, because God's love has been poured into our hearts through the Holy Spirit who has been given to us.

The resurrection also fulfills prophecies from many years earlier. Isaiah 25:8 states that "He will swallow up death forever. The Sovereign Lord will wipe away the tears from all faces." In Isaiah 53:5, we read, "But he was pierced for our transgressions, he was crushed for our iniquities; the punishment that brought us peace was on him, and by his wounds we are healed."

Perhaps in due course, like Jesus, you too will see victory on earth. Perhaps it's a different job, a better situation and justice against perpetrators. If that happens, then great!

Maybe we won't see such an outcome on earth. Take hope that Jesus' death has made heaven possible. Remember the power of his death to wipe away the tears from our deepest pains because of what awaits. Realize that we can experience everlasting healing from his wounds.

In thinking about redemption, Jesus' death and resurrection also relates to the professional who has secured achievements but still feels dissatisfaction. Belief in the death and resurrection of Jesus offers the ultimate connection to God. No temporary workplace achievement or success can compare to this.

I can think of no gift that provides the ultimate peace and motivation, even in the midst of career disappointments and frustrations. If you don't adhere to the Christian faith, I pray that this reality might be an entryway for you to consider the power of the gospel message that you may have previously overlooked. For all of us, may this gift empower us to do our best and most impactful work here on earth, knowing that a greater prize awaits.

Zoom Out on the Realities of Your Environment

Here are some questions and points to consider (ideally to discuss with a friend or in a small group).

- Is there someone who has betrayed you or wronged you at work? If yes, do you still have anger or resentment towards this person? How can you muster the strength to genuinely forgive this person?

- What can we learn from Christ about what it takes to forgive someone who has wronged us?

- How do you think the promise of heaven and eternity with Christ can impact your approach to dealing with workplace difficulties?

PART II

ANGLES TO AVOID

Principle #5: Career Idealism

Hopefully, considering the realities covered in the first four principles is helping you to think differently about career success. It is also important to be aware of two specific career-related pitfalls. The first one is career idealism.

I've been running my own communications consulting company since 2013 and have collaborated with a range of different clients from around the world. There is one constant refrain I hear from these clients: Someone isn't happy. So many rank-and-file employees have shared with me their disenchantment with work. Disgruntled leaders often communicate their frustrations.

Career dissatisfaction is also reflected in different research studies. More than 14,000 employees, managers, HR leaders and c-level executives across 13 countries took part in a 2021 survey led by Oracle and Workplace Intelligence.[26] Key findings include:

- 75% feel stuck professionally because they:
    - don't have growth opportunities to progress their careers (25%); and
    - are too overwhelmed to make any changes (22%);
- 70% say that feeling stuck in their career has negatively impacted their personal lives as well by:
    - adding extra stress and anxiety (40%);
    - contributing to feeling stuck personally (29%); and
    - taking focus away from their personal lives (27%);

- 83% are ready to make a change, but 76% said they are facing major obstacles.

That is an overwhelming number of dissatisfied people. Do you resonate with the majority? Talk to your peer groups and ask if they are satisfied with their work. My guess is that you will find similar trends.

I was wondering… Are only recent generations so disgruntled at work? Or were previous generations also unenthused about their work? It is hard to know concretely, as the term "employee engagement" was only introduced in 1990 in an Academy of Management Journal article.[27]

Here's my guess: My late grandfathers would have no idea what employee engagement and satisfaction meant or why it was important. Many in the boomer generation would probably say the same thing. These generations didn't approach work thinking about how they could glean satisfaction. If employee engagement were measured 50 to 75 years ago, my guess would be that their scores would be higher. Work was much more of an exchange, particularly for those in the industrial economy. Work = paycheck.

This transactional approach to work isn't optimal. I also think that organizations are smart to consider how to best engage employees. But I believe that much of the current discourse around careers—from the messages shared with college students to the content that working professionals consume in the media—has caused us to become too idealistic about our careers, leading to low engagement.

The previous generations weren't fed a narrative that accomplishments were tied to happiness and their work would contribute to grandiose ideas of self-importance. As part of this shift away from transactional work, many today are being sold a false story that our identity comes from work.

Generations before us also weren't bombarded with people's work highlights on social media. Many today only see the glory and not the hard work, sweat, tears and suffering in the same social media post. There is an unspoken assumption that we are entitled to such positive experiences.

Accept the Realities of Painful Toil

Perhaps many today have forgotten that we live in a fallen world in which things don't always go according to plan. We are told in the Genesis account that, as a result of sin, work will involve "painful toil" and will be characterized by "thorns and thistles." We often fail to remember that people do harm to one another for their own selfish gain. We are naive to the fact that events beyond our control unfold, impacting our daily work and future plans. Our time on earth isn't going to be a walk in the park.

> We need to remember that painful toil is part of the work experience and that there is a season for everything.

Another principle that can be helpful in dealing with the harsh realities that work can be difficult is the idea of seasons. According to Ecclesiastes 3:1–2:

> There is a time for everything,
> and a season for every activity under heaven:
> a time to be born and a time to die,
> a time to plant and a time to uproot,

The chapter goes on to detail a number of different positive and negative life situations that many face. The idea that our time on earth won't be an entirely rosy experience is also highlighted in various sections of the New Testament. For example, Romans 8:18–22 says:

> I consider that our present sufferings are not worth comparing with the glory that will be revealed in us. For the creation waits in eager expectation for the children of God to be revealed. For the creation was subjected to frustration, not by its own choice, but by the will of the one who subjected it, in hope that the creation itself will be liberated from its bondage to decay and brought into the freedom and glory of the children of God. We know that the whole creation has been groaning as in the pains of childbirth right up to the present time.

Very few people, even the most powerful and influential (from an earthly perspective) would state that their plans went according to plan. We need to remember that painful toil is part of the work experience and that there is a season for everything. If we can be prepared to accept this reality, then when a disappointment comes along, we won't be completely upended. We can have peace that the storm will eventually pass. We can be motivated that, as a result of whatever friction and disappointment we face, we can come out stronger in different ways.

Rethink Buzzwords and Phrases

We are told a whole host of glorious career development buzzwords and phrases. Much of this lingo can lead us down a path of career fantasy wonderland. When the dream doesn't become reality, it can result in disillusionment, frustration and anger.

For example, we are encouraged to "pursue our passions." On the surface, this is good advice. We certainly don't want to be working in unmotivating jobs. We will work harder and create more of an impact if our career paths are aligned to our interests and skills. However, my hunch is that there is a misinterpretation around "passion" as providing complete individual satisfaction. We usually associate the word passion from a romance perspective. As it relates to careers, passion becomes about fulfilling individual, usually self-serving goals. When self-serving career passions don't pan out as expected, many tend to react like an emotional teenager who was rejected by someone they were interested in romantically.

To counter this, I think it is important to instill definitions and parameters for ourselves. For the purpose of this book, infusing a faith-based perspective into these definitions is recommended. So, for passion, we can use a definition like a "vocation leading to joy both for oneself and others." Think about vocational passion in these terms, and the related goals might look different than taking the term passion at face value, which usually veers into personal satisfaction.

We are encouraged to pursue work that "will change the world." Consider the following possible definitions of this work:

A. Starting a worldwide movement that is globally recognized; or
B. Helping one neighbor, client or colleague in need, which changes that person's life trajectory.

Many, especially younger people, would answer "A." In reality, making a difference in the world could mean that you launch a national movement around countering climate change and that the topic propels you to be the president of your country. But it could also mean that your passion for natural preservation leads you to a career in teaching, and you influence a small number of students each year.

On the surface of it, the president made far more of a difference than the educator. However, I believe that in God's eyes, both could have made an equal difference. With God, numbers alone are not the metric used for judging a person's impact. Maybe it is possible that the educator made more of a difference while the president was making decisions to preserve power as opposed to truly wanting to make a difference around conservation matters.

Similarly, let's look at the term "extraordinary" and consider it through the lens of healthcare. You can be extraordinary and find the cure for cancer. At the same time, nurses can be extraordinary by providing exceptional care for each individual patient they encounter who is suffering.

Career coaches have great content that helps people find their "dream job." Think about those two words. A dream coming true conjures up ideas of our wildest ideas becoming reality. It is like when we are sleeping and have that amazing dream and almost feel disappointment when we wake up. That narrative in our discourse usually doesn't reveal the realities of this myth: Every profession, even the most glorious ones, includes plenty of hardships and annoyances.

As a kid, I thought a dream job would be working as a professional athlete. The prospects of getting paid lots of money to play a sport in front of adoring fans sounded too good to be true. Ask athletes like Tiger Woods if that is, indeed, the case. The documentary on Tiger Woods' life shows a person who has been troubled in various ways, from the pressure of living up to expectations to the inconveniences of never being able to go out publicly without being hounded by fans and media. There are also the mundane aspects of the job—the countless hours lifting weights or fine-tuning the technical aspect of a sport.

Downsides exist for every profession, regardless of one's title or role. As we define what our dream career looks like, let's remember these realities of working in a fallen world.

We are told to work for "purpose-driven organizations" whose mission and values align to our own belief system. That is a very nice idea. We can read beautiful language under the "About" section of a company's website and feel connected to the brand. But what happens when we see the brand or individuals working for the organization behaving differently than what is so eloquently stated on the website? Talk is wonderful. Actions are more difficult, and we can easily become disillusioned when we experience this disconnect. Be realistic in seeking opportunities to collaborate or work for a "purpose-driven organization" in a fallen world.

As you think about your career-related definitions, be cognizant of Christ's grace for us. Many of us approach work in a capitalistic way. We perform and deliver value for our organizations or directly for customers and clients, and then, as a result, some type of reward is bestowed upon us. Those of us who live and work in a capitalistic society should rightfully work from this mindset of tying benefits to performance.

However, we must remember that the ultimate spiritual reward—salvation—is the antithesis to this capitalistic approach. The Christian worldview teaches that we are not saved by our performance. The grace of God is bestowed upon us as a gift through accepting that Christ died to forgive the sins of all. As we embark on our career journeys, we can have peace that this outcome doesn't impact our complete identity. We can remain motivated in our work, knowing that we can only do our best as humanly possible, but that we are accepted and loved regardless.

Angles to Avoid

Here are some questions and points to consider (ideally to discuss with a friend or in a small group).

- Think back to a painful career experience. How did you respond? At the time, did you consider the ideas of painful toil and that there is a season for everything? If you did, how did this impact your response? If you didn't, do you think you would have responded differently if you had taken into account this reality?

- Are there steps you can take to avoid "career idealism" so that you will be better prepared for the next inevitable professional setback?

- How would you define, ideally with an eternal lens, vocational terms like:
  - Making a difference
  - Pursuing your passion
  - Extraordinary
  - (Add other terms as you deem necessary)

- How do you connect your values and beliefs to imperfect organizations?

Principle #6: Workplace Idols

On your deathbed, will you regret not having spent enough time at work? You may have heard some version of this question posed before. Most everybody—even the most super ambitious executive to the creative and dynamic entrepreneur—would agree that this won't be one of our regrets. You can imagine that common regrets shared on deathbeds usually center on family, friends and the afterlife (regardless of one's religion). Yet, we frequently don't live this way.

We also know that when we die, God will not care, per se, about the power we have accrued at work or the money we have in our bank account. Richard Stearns, former CEO of Lenox, Parker Brothers Games and World Vision, wrote about this in the book *Lead Like It Matters to God: Values-Driven Leadership in a Success-Driven World*:

> Despite my three CEO titles and decades of working in multiple organizations, I just can't imagine God saying to me: "Well done, good and faithful servant, for those twenty consecutive quarters of earnings growth!" or, "Way to go, Rich, on becoming a CEO at the age of thirty-three. You killed it!" No, I don't think God will be impressed by those things. Hey, my wife isn't even impressed by those things. It's far more likely that God will speak to us about how we led and how we lived.[28]

Many people, especially Christians, would agree with this perspective. However, we often don't live like this. Consider what you think about during your down time. What would you guess is the ratio of career pursuits to other aspects of life?

Think about when you are at a new social gathering, and you meet someone for the first time. How long does it take before someone asks, "What do you do for a living?" That is usually one of our first questions. If we think this person's work is in some way beneficial to us, we stick around and chat. If it isn't so interesting, we often sheepishly say that we need another drink and sneak away.

Of course, there is nothing wrong per se with thinking about our work and career goals in our down time. Nor is there anything bad about asking a person what they do for a living and finding that we might click with one individual as opposed to another based on common professional interests. The problem is that we often overvalue career identities, both in ourselves and others, at the expense of so many other important areas of life.

Derek Thompson, a writer for *The Atlantic* and not necessarily someone who purports to any particular faith to my knowledge, captured this poignantly in his article titled "Workism Is Making Americans Miserable":

> The decline of traditional faith in America has coincided with an explosion of new atheisms. Some people worship beauty, some worship political identities, and others worship their children. But everybody worships something. And workism is among the most potent of the new religions competing for congregants.
>
> What is workism? It is the belief that work is not only necessary to economic production, but also the centerpiece of one's identity and life's purpose; and the belief that any policy to promote human welfare must *always* encourage more work.[29]

Having lived and worked in Europe for 10 years, I think this analysis also applies to those from many other countries—not just Americans.

So many of us are guilty of prioritizing our work and career over other areas of life. In his book, *The Road to Character*, David Brooks wrote:

> The résumé virtues are the ones you list on your résumé, the skills that you bring to the job market and that contribute to external success. The eulogy virtues are deeper. They're the virtues that get talked about at your funeral, the ones that exist at the core of your being—whether you are kind, brave, honest or faithful; what kind of relationships you formed.
>
> Most of us would say that the eulogy virtues are more important than the résumé virtues, but I confess that for long stretches of my life I've spent more time thinking about the latter than the former. Our education system is certainly oriented around the résumé virtues more than the eulogy ones. Public conversation is, too—the self-help tips in magazines, the nonfiction bestsellers. Most of us have clearer strategies for how to achieve career success than we do for how to develop a profound character.[30]

The longing for career accomplishment can be quite a trap. In a Faith and Work public lecture, Regent College professor S. Paul Stevens noted that work reveals a personal point of weakness that is usually related to our need to be needed, our need to be approved or our need to be in control.[31]

On the surface of it, achievement is great. We need to work and succeed in our jobs to make a living for ourselves and contribute to society in whatever large or small ways. Our world needs exceptionally talented surgeons to help cure people of sickness. CEOs need to lead their organizations to profitability so that their goods and services can benefit others and sustain the livelihood of employees. Entrepreneurs need to come up with innovative and marketable ideas to grow their businesses.

Such accomplishments should be appreciated and celebrated—within reason and with perspective. We are bombarded with the notion of achievement from an early age. We try to work according to whatever standard we have established in our minds. Usually, there isn't much critical thinking involved.

Another dynamic contributing to career priority unbalance is social media. Consider the allure of YouTube fame that has seeped into the consciousnesses of children. In a survey conducted by Harris Poll on behalf of Lego, children in the United States and the United Kingdom were three times as likely to want to be YouTubers or vloggers as astronauts when they grow up.[32]

In a separate study conducted by the UK-based travel company, First Choice, three quarters of children say they would consider some sort of career in online videos.[33] The biggest attractions noted were creativity, fame and the opportunity for self-expression, with money trailing in fourth place.

The Fleeting Nature of Our Career Legacies

Career success is fleeting. This reality is overlooked in our career achievement discourse. Think about your answer to this question: What do you want your career legacy to be? It is an important question to consider. I think how we might answer this question is far more grandiose than what is very likely.

Imagine that it is 150 years from now. It is the decade of the 2170s. Let's keep in mind that 150 years, in comparison to the history of the world, is actually a very short amount of time. Here is an educated guess about the realities of our career legacies.

The Organizations Where We Spent the Most Years Will Be Extinct

Think about the organization where you have dedicated the most time throughout your career. I would venture to say that very few of these organizations were around 150 years ago, in the 1870s. This will likely be the case 150 years in the future as well.

McKinsey & Company found that the average lifespan of companies listed in Standard & Poor's 500 was 61 years in 1958.[34] Today, it is less than 18 years. If you look at lists of the most influential companies in the 1800s, you will primarily see organizations that were in the industrial space.

Look at today's powerful companies, such as Amazon, Facebook and Netflix. These organizations all began in the last 25 years. In our "enlightened times," we might be inclined to believe that the amazing innovations these and other organizations have brought to the market will be long-lasting. That is what Blockbuster and Kodak probably assumed before their businesses were upended. There is a reasonable chance that companies like Amazon, Facebook and Netflix will be extinct in 150 years. That could be the reality for the company where you work as well. If your goal is to have a lasting legacy that will propel your organization for centuries to come, you might want to reconsider some of your priorities.

Our Jobs, in All Likelihood, Won't Even Exist

Think about the decade of the 1870s. Did your job exist? Many of the lists of most common jobs involved laborers. Now, think about the 2170s. Will your job exist? Google the "future of work," and you will see countless articles on how artificial intelligence and automation will disrupt jobs and industries. Many have already seen this play out. Just ask travel agents and transcriptionists.

If your goal is to have a lasting legacy within your industry, you might want to reconsider some of your priorities. There is a chance that your industry won't even exist in 150 years.

Nobody Will Remember You

Sorry to disappoint, but it is true. Your colleagues and those you influence on a regular basis today will all be dead. Can you name your great, great grandparents? What about their best career achievements? If you struggle with these questions, how can you expect your great, great grandchildren to remember your name and career achievements?

Let's look at today's stars. In 2022, Jeff Bezos and Elon Musk are the top two richest people in the world. Who was the richest man in the world some 150 years ago? Wikipedia tells me it was Cornelius Vanderbilt.[35] How much does his legacy impact you today? My guess is not at all. (If you are associated with Vanderbilt University, you might answer this question differently.)

Novak Djokovic is at the top of the tennis world today. Who was the top tennis champion from 150 years ago? Most of the sports we watch today weren't even in existence at a professional level back then.

Let's go to the world of entertainment. Over the last few years, many have religiously followed the plight of Britney Spears' conservatorship battle and the everyday actions of the Kardashians. Who were the top entertainers from the 1870s?

If the people at the very top of their professions are forgotten, then the harsh reality is that nobody will remember you, let alone your professional successes (and failures).

It bears repeating: 150 years, in comparison to the history of the world, is actually a very short amount of time. Go back 1000, 2000 and 3000 years ago, and you will find that the above points are not very different.

Awareness of Success Idols Provides Peace and Motivation

I actually think this reality about forgotten career legacies can be freeing. When we take the pressure off ourselves, we can think about how our individual contributions can potentially impact our families and communities long after we have died and our names are forgotten.

While nobody will remember your individual successes and failures, your career performances are able to influence generations. If my great grandparents hadn't emigrated from Italy to the US in the early 1900s, I would have been raised in Sicily. (Not a bad proposition, mind you.) The hard work of my forefathers and foremothers helped make it possible for me to be the first in my family to graduate from college. I don't know anything really about these distant relatives, but their contributions paved the way for me and many others after them.

Then there is the focus on community. While our individual glories (and failures) will be forgotten, the contributions can

64

leave a legacy in the community. Take the Federal Aid Highway Act of 1956 in the United States that led to the formation of the current highway system. We probably can't name one person who actually constructed those highways in the late 1950s. But most of us in our communities benefit from those efforts today.

Let's imagine that a construction worker named Joe wanted his legacy to be known for painting the yellow dividing lines on highways during the 1950s. Well, Joe would be disappointed to know that his individual efforts were forgotten. If his motivation had been to enable his and future generations to travel more efficiently, then he would have been able to take satisfaction in the results of the project. (Joe is probably dead today, but you get the point!)

For Christians, connecting the spiritual as part of our career legacy enables us to work with a greater eternal perspective. Using the highway example, we can assume that, decades into the future, the highways we currently use will not be around. Maybe there will be a new highway system, or roads won't be necessary as we will all be flying around in electric planes or using robots. If we think about our work as a contribution at one specific point in time as part of a higher being's master plan, we can take satisfaction in our work. If we are so obsessed with our individual contributions, then it can be depressing to think about how our contributions are not only forgotten but also useless in the future. This applies to all professions.

It impacts how we treat one another too. If we are only after our individual glory as part of our legacy, then we will make whatever ruthless decisions to advance that agenda. If we have a realistic approach to our career legacies—that our individual successes and failures will be forgotten—we can

> Humans will die, and individuals will be forgotten, so working solely to please our fellow man will result inevitably in letdowns.

then treat people differently. We can realize that how we treat our fellow human beings, who happen to be on the earth at the same time we are in this particular moment in time, should take a much higher precedence over advancing our individual agendas. When we realize that loving and caring for our neighbors in need has more eternal value than working 120 hours a week to earn a promotion, we can refocus our priorities on how we treat each other.

One possible misinterpretation of our forgotten career legacies is that our work doesn't matter. As a Christian, I would say that is quite the contrary. The Apostle Paul writes in Colossians 3:23–24, "Whatever you do, work at it with all your heart, as working for the Lord, not for human masters, since you know that you will receive an inheritance from the Lord as a reward. It is the Lord Christ you are serving." Humans will die, and individuals will be forgotten, so working solely to please our fellow man will result inevitably in letdowns. But working for an eternal God comes with an even greater responsibility.

Bosses on earth—whether a direct supervisor, a board, our customers or clients—primarily evaluate our work deliverables. Sure, there are many bosses who care about our well-being too. But most of us have come to realize that, when we transition from one organization to another, everything moves on. These bosses' priorities shift to the next person.

For the "eternal boss," work is just one aspect of our callings on earth. We are also to be faithful as it relates to how we grow in our personal relationship with God, how we care for our families and how we engage with our communities. It becomes very easy to sacrifice these other responsibilities for the sake of our career fulfillment. In addition, the more we experience temporary satisfaction through our work accomplishments, the easier it is to overlook the need for God in our lives. Consider Ecclesiastes 2:21–22:

> For a person may labor with wisdom, knowledge and skill, and then they must leave all they own to another who has not toiled for it. This too is meaningless and a great misfortune. What do people get for all the toil and anxious striving with which they labor under the sun?

In the New Testament (Matthew 6:19–20), Jesus warned:

> Do not store up for yourselves treasures on earth, where moths and vermin destroy, and where thieves break in and steal. But store up for yourselves treasures in heaven, where moths and vermin do not destroy, and where thieves do not break in and steal.

When asked about the greatest commandment, Jesus said to love God and others as yourself. A desirable legacy of one's work is usually more about how you interacted with your co-workers or employees than the work you actually did. Think back on positive key turning points in your career. You can probably recall individuals' characteristics more than the actual projects you worked on.

We live at a point in time in which there is more focus on the individual than at any time in history. Because of this, it is difficult to recalibrate and put our legacies and the false idol of career success into perspective. At least, that is the case for me. Let's think through these realities and adjust as needed. If we do so, we can grapple with career disappointments and work towards future goals with greater peace and motivation.

Angles to Avoid

Here are some questions and points to consider (ideally to discuss with a friend or in a small group).

- What do you think of your career legacy?

- How can the Christian message help shape your perspective?

- How might you work differently as you consider the realities of your career legacy? Should you approach a particular project or role in a new way?

PART III

ZOOMING IN
ON THE DETAILS
OF YOUR CAREER
SUCCESS PICTURE

Principle #7: Define Your Career Success

Succinctly defining career success is difficult, regardless of one's faith. As a Christian, I find it particularly challenging in part because of how we have misconstrued the idea of God's blessings and the overall false message of gospel prosperity. The belief is that those who approach God in faith and obedience will experience wealth, health and power.[36]

Sometimes, this false gospel prosperity message is obvious to detect, such as when we see immaculately dressed televangelists flying around on their private jets proclaiming that their fortunes are the result of their faith and actions. In other instances, it is more subtle and unintentionally deceptive.

For example, one day in 2021, I was feeling particularly down about a project that wasn't going according to plan. I had a conversation with a friend. This person shared with me how he had made Christ the center of his company and, as a result, had been "blessed" with a significant uptick in business compared to the past year.

"Great," I thought to myself. "So, God has 'blessed' this person with success around his business. Why am I not receiving the favor of God for my project?"

Perhaps you have asked yourself a similar question at different low points in your career, and this has altered your viewpoint about what success entails. Before working on your career success definition, it is important to unpack the idea of blessings and career success (or lack thereof). Here are four points to consider.

1. We Have Misconstrued the Definition of Blessing

To begin with, what does *blessing* mean? Many social media humble brag posts suggest that a blessing is a nice little prize—such as a pay raise or professional recognition—from God as the result of our marvelous wonders. You will surely find many out there who claim that this is, indeed, what a blessing entails (perhaps expressed a tad more eloquently).

Some base this rationale on the lives of wealthy individuals from the Old Testament, such as David, Job, Solomon and Joseph. Indeed, these were people who accumulated influence and possessions. But prosperity gospel advocates fail to take into account the different nuances between the Old and New Testaments.

In very broad strokes, the Old Testament points to the life of Jesus Christ. The New Testament details the life of Jesus and explains how belief that he is the Son of God and died for our sins is the basis for salvation. It is through his grace alone, not individual works, that believers experience the benefits of salvation. There is an apparent shift from material blessing in the Old Testament to spiritual blessing in the New Testament.

The books of the Christian New Testament are widely agreed to have originally been written in Greek. The Greek word for blessing is *makarioi*, which means to be fully satisfied. It refers to those receiving God's favor, regardless of the circumstances. Even the almighty modern answer to all our questions—Google—reinforces this definition, noting that "blessed" as an adjective is being "made holy; consecrated." The noun form is "those who live in heaven with God."

In an article entitled "Prosperity a Blessing," Daniel Boerman noted that the word blessing appears 44 times in the New Testament. In 31 of those instances, the blessing relates to righteous behavior or characteristics that God considers desirable.[37] According to his analysis, there is not one time when the word blessing is associated with material prosperity. I don't think this is a coincidence!

> It is somewhat blasphemous to hijack the idea of God's blessings to make it fit our own career success agendas.

The most famous reference to the word *blessed* are the Beatitudes preached by Jesus Christ along the Sea of Galilee. Those who are blessed, according to Jesus, are the poor in spirit, those who mourn, the meek, those who hunger and thirst for righteousness, the merciful, the pure in heart, the peacemakers and those who are persecuted because of righteousness. The second reference to each blessing has a spiritual reward—like "blessed are the merciful, for they will be shown mercy"; or "blessed are the pure in heart, for they will see God." Jesus could have said they will get job promotions, accumulate great material wealth and gain professional fame for living out some of these principles. But he didn't, because it is not necessarily what a blessing entails.

"Scripture shows that blessing is anything God gives that makes us fully satisfied in him," wrote Vaneetha Rendall Risner for the blog *Desiring God*. "Anything that draws us closer to Jesus. Anything that helps us relinquish the temporal and hold on more tightly to the eternal. And often it is the struggles and trials, the aching disappointments and the unfulfilled longings that best enable us to do that."[38]

It is somewhat blasphemous to hijack the idea of God's blessings to make it fit our own career success agendas. The gospel of Christ is about getting something—salvation and spiritual connection, the ultimate blessing—through faith and grace. This is quite different from insinuating that our actions lead to career résumé boosters.

Sadly, much of the Christian discourse over the last few decades has skewed to this version of a gospel that offers personal success. You can see this on display in books, articles and even in "worship" songs.

2. If Financial Abundance Is God's Blessing, Why Do Many Horrible People Have So Much?

By many accounts, Osama Bin Laden, mastermind of the 9/11 attacks, was a wealthy man. He was the heir to a Saudi billionaire and had a fortune widely estimated at $300 million.[39]

At the time of this writing, Vladimir Putin is bringing death and destruction to the people of Ukraine. His net worth is a mystery. Some wonder if he is actually the wealthiest person alive today.[40]

These are two of many examples of individuals who accumulated significant power and wealth and brought about great harm to others. Which begs the question: If whatever career success you accumulated is due to God's blessing you for your actions, why are these bad people being "blessed" as well?

3. It Could Be Offensive to Others

Think about this example. Two people climb up a mountain. An avalanche occurs, and both climbers go missing. Eventually, one person is found to have survived, while the other has perished.

The family of the survivor is jubilant and thanks God for the blessing of protection. The grieving family of the victim watches in another room. How do you think they feel? What are they thinking about the words of the surviving climber's family members? What questions are they asking of God? How could a just God bless one person with protection and not the other person? I would say with certainty that the words used by the surviving family are offensive. I would also argue that their analysis is not necessarily true because, as previously covered, nobody knows God's specific intentions.

Life vs. death and career success vs. failure are obviously two separate matters. But think about a person who was fired unjustly from a job. How do you think that individual feels when conversing with someone who just received a promotion and attributes it to God's blessings?

4. We Fall into the Trap of Wrongfully Proclaiming God's Motives

When we go out of our way to proclaim God's blessings on us, we risk "getting out of our lane" by proclaiming the motives of our all-knowing God as His children.

Consider this analogy. In 2017, my family and I moved from one house to another in Chapel Hill, North Carolina. My sons were four and six years old at the time. They didn't have the maturity, experience or wisdom to begin to hypothesize why my wife and I made this decision. It would have been crazy if they met friends and provided thoughtful analysis on the pros and cons of the two different neighborhoods.

Yet, when we proclaim that our actions have led to God's blessings, we are essentially acting like young children analyzing important adult decisions. I actually think that there is a greater gap between human adults analyzing the motives of God than children doing the same with their parents' decisions.

Isaiah 55:8–9 states, "For my thoughts are not your thoughts, neither are your ways my ways," declares the Lord. "As the heavens are higher than the earth, so are my ways higher than your ways and my thoughts than your thoughts." We don't need to make proclamations, declaring who God allots blessings to. Let's stay in our lanes as human beings.

Thinking Differently About Blessings and Career Outcomes

I should mention that wishing God's blessing on a couple at their wedding or to share this phrase to a grieving family is a completely different usage and application. In this case, it aligns to the intended Christian principle of God's blessing— being fully satisfied in God, regardless of the circumstances. There are other scenarios that would probably be appropriate as well.

While every good gift does indeed come from God, I suggest that we eliminate from our vocabulary the phrase "so blessed" when speaking of our own career successes. It is just too easy to have the wrong motivation when we use the dreadful humble brag hashtag #SoBlessed in our social media posts.

At the same time, I also hope that the above perspectives might help you think differently about any career disappointments and successes vis-à-vis your relationship to God. If it is a disappointment, maybe whatever you are encountering is a temporary valley. Perhaps one scenario is that you will come out on the other side and achieve the goal and learn a whole lot in the process. I hope this happens for you. Success and achievement are certainly positive when the recipient is faithful and responsible in stewarding earthly gifts. The other scenario is that your career aspiration won't ever come to fruition. Maybe there is a different path you are intended to go down.

Whatever happens, may you realize that the real blessings emanating from Christ's sacrificial love have nothing to do with whatever scenario occurs. We all have the opportunity to experience Christ's actual blessings, whether we are millionaires reaping the joys of earthly career success or unemployed and grappling with career disappointments.

Characterizing Your Career Success

Now that we have explored what actual blessings entail, let's zoom in further on what career success means for you. Success is a word that we think about from our youth. We throw the term around continually, but many fail to define it. We typically associate career success with money, influence, prestige and power.

As a Christian, I believe success could entail these outcomes. However, there is an important caveat. If such outcomes came about through unethical means—exploiting others, being dishonest or behaving irresponsibly—then it is difficult for me to consider them a success. Ditto if outcomes lead to feelings of superiority over others, a sense of entitlement and the failure to appropriately use the money, influence, prestige and power in a positive way.

For me, other keywords and phrases that embody career success as a Christian include:

- Faithfulness
- Being wise and responsible financially so we are not dependent on others
- Using our gifts and talents to the best of our ability
- Learning and depending on God in all circumstances
- Being an ambassador for Christ with the means we have been provided
- Serving others instead of ourselves
- Generating the maximum impact according to the Lord's will

To give a practical example, let me define what success looks like for this book.

If the Lord wills, my goal is to use the book as a springboard to shift the focus of my consulting work. I would love to share the content of this book by leading workshops and coaching others. Over the 20 plus years of my professional life, I have accrued different skills and a network that I think can help amplify the messages of this book. I believe that it would be unwise for me to write this book and not use the talents God has given me to spread the message. So, I do have some very concrete goals set up and am executing a marketing strategy to try to accomplish them.

But, if the Lord wills that the only person to ever read this book is me, I will still consider it a success. I will accept that it was meant for me to write this book for my own learning—which, in fact, has been a very powerful and deeply spiritual experience. I will also draw inspiration from the countless people noted in the Bible whose names were not recorded but who played a part in the Gospel story.

Let's imagine that I am obsessed with reaching certain sales goals around this book, and that becomes my sole metric for success. If this doesn't happen, I might become distraught by my failure and sense that I am not being "blessed" as it is interpreted in everyday discourse. However, with the ideas of blessing as described in this chapter, I can take satisfaction *regardless of the outcome*.

Thinking through blessings and success with this lens provides me with peace and motivation. If the book is read by just one other person, I can hope that, perhaps, this individual will think about God and work differently. That person might never pay attention to the author of this book but may act on the points above and approach work differently than he or she may have in the past. I might not ever see or be aware of the impact, whether big or small. As opposed to being upset that just two people read this book, I can take satisfaction in rethinking the success of this project, knowing God is at work even when I can't see or understand it.

It is advisable to think about career success definitions for both projects (like this book) and one's work overall. Definitions should take into account the principles covered in this book. For me, my definition of overall career success looks like this:

- I am a child of God. I will do my work with integrity.
- Education (the sector in which I primarily work) and wisdom are important for the flourishing of this world. I will do my work with excellence, not for personal glory

but to contribute my part to advancing knowledge at this given point in time.

- I am to financially provide and care for my family through my work. I will continually look for ways to increase my income and impact as the Lord wills and look to give back as I am able.
- The gospel message provides everlasting peace. I will look to advance that message through this book project and in building relationships as part of my work.

Each of these points has two parts. First, I wrote a fact and followed it with a second statement addressing what I can do in response as part of my work. I also want this to be short and memorable so that it truly serves as a guide for daily decision-making and action. As I embark on this definition of career success, I keep in mind that my identity and value doesn't come from career outcomes!

Zoom In on the Details of Your Career Success Picture

Now, it is your turn. I hope that this content serves as a springboard for you to define career success with a Christian perspective, whether for your overall work or for a specific project. My personal example isn't all-encompassing, so feel free to make it your own. God leads and convicts each person to think about what career success means with an eternal gospel-oriented perspective.

Perhaps you feel that it is too difficult to craft your career success definition. It helps to start somewhere, so I strongly encourage you to write out some ideas before moving on to the next chapter. Don't worry if it isn't the most eloquent career success definition. You can fine-tune this later. Conversations with others will also provide more clarity and perspective. Please take action now and write out your initial thoughts to these questions.

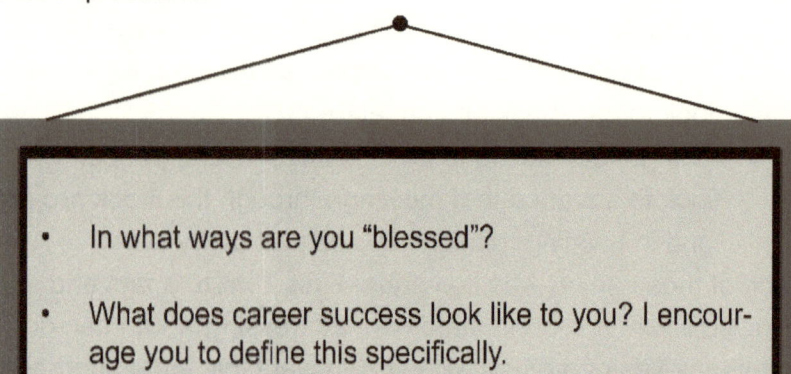

- In what ways are you "blessed"?

- What does career success look like to you? I encourage you to define this specifically.

- How can you apply your definition to any current work circumstances?

Principle #8: Write Out Your Metrics

Hopefully, you now have some initial ideas about your definition of career success. Building on this, consider different metrics related to your definition. To clarify the semantics, I have as part of my career success definition that I will do my work with integrity. A related metric is ensuring that all business write-offs are legitimate and to err on the side of not expensing items in the gray zone.

For your inspiration, I wanted to share with you three very different examples of individuals who have unique perspectives on career success metrics.

Example 1: An Ambassador for Christ

If you check out the LinkedIn profile of Miles Veth, you will see the following words in his title: "Christ-Follower | CEO @ Veth Group." Scroll down and his LinkedIn About paragraph states: "I am a follower of Jesus Christ, and my professional goal is to honor him in the way I do business. I run Veth Group. We are experts at B2B appointment setting...." The summary then highlights the company's profile.

I was always struck by how Miles made Christ the center of his business, which consists of 15+ employees, including his wife. It was interesting to hear the genesis of how he decided to be more open about his faith. He had just started his own company and was achieving success in terms of client work and traction with his LinkedIn content.

One day, he shared a LinkedIn post about business development email templates. The post was a hit and generated 1.7 million views. While this was gratifying, a reality dawned on Miles that none of these individuals viewing the post would know that Christ was important to him. At the same time, Miles was reading about Jim Elliott, the American missionary who was killed in 1956 at the age of 28 as a result of his evangelistic activities in Ecuador.

"I got to thinking that if others could be so bold in their faith to risk their lives, then I could be bolder in sharing my faith while safely running my business," Miles said.

Hence, Miles decided to take action and communicate his faith via his LinkedIn profile and other outlets. Many have responded favorably, while others haven't appreciated his stances, resulting in unpleasant messages. One company even refused to work with him on account of his boldness. Miles doesn't mind.

"Matthew 16:24 tells us that we should take up our cross and follow him. There should be a price to pay," he said.

For Miles, his goal of building a God-honoring business that is distinctively Christian means that:

- There is a giving mindset: 10 percent of all company profits are given away to help others;
- The company is doing pro bono work around important causes; and
- He aims to treat clients and employees differently.

This God-honoring business mindset impacts how he handles adversity. As cliché as it sounds, he's come to see obstacles as opportunities to bring God glory and display his faith in Jesus, despite setbacks.

"My prayer is that God uses me to bring him glory even when things don't go as I would like," he said. "It is easy to say 'woe is me' when things don't go according to plan. But, in reality, woe is Paul and so many others who gave up their lives for Jesus. When you look at it from this perspective, it is laughable."

I asked Miles what he would want others to say about his career. His answer: "I am less interested in earthly goal setting. Numbers can deceive. I want people to recognize that it was God who provided, not me. I want to be remembered as someone who followed Jesus."

Example 2: "Keep Us Small and Unknown"

From what I understand, many churches evaluate their success by the ABCs: attendance, buildings and cash. Meet Su Slack, wife of Martin Slack, pastor of Westlake, an international English-speaking church located in Lausanne, Switzerland (the French-speaking part of the country).

Su says a regular prayer that is diametrically at odds with these ABCs. The prayer goes something like this: "Keep us small and unknown." That is not a typo. And, no, Su doesn't pray for the church to be unsuccessful. Her aspiration isn't that the church will be a flop and have no impact. It is actually the contrary.

Martin and Su believe that one of their key criteria for success should be based around caring for others (among other points). Hence, on any given Sunday, the Slacks will be hosting a lunch at their house with different members and visitors who are primarily expats working in the region and students attending different schools and universities. For four years, I had the opportunity to be part of many of those joyous meals.

"There is a fixation on fame and making a name for oneself," said Martin. "If you achieve this, it leads to pride. If you don't, it can cause you despair. For Su and me, it would fundamentally hinder what true success means for us, which is Christ likeness and caring for the people God has brought to us. Using the wrong metrics of success brings temptations that endanger progress towards the real metric of success, which is Christ likeness."

When I asked what he would do if he showed up to his church doors and found 2,000 people there instead of 250, Martin had a great response. "There was a mix-up on Google maps, and these people must have the wrong address," he quipped. After my laughter subsided, he shared, "I would pray for grace and ask for forgiveness for any pride."

> "There is a fixation on fame and making a name for oneself. If you achieve this, it leads to pride. If you don't, it can cause you despair."

Martin is quick to point out that the goals he and Su have for the church are not a judgment on bigger churches. For the Slacks, they can take great joy in influencing a few at a very deep and personal level. That is part of their calling.

These are certainly counterintuitive metrics for a pastor and his wife. Though it probably shouldn't come as a surprise, considering the Slacks' career journey. Both Su and Martin held the well-respected title of doctor and practiced medicine in the United Kingdom for many years. They were working in their dream jobs but ultimately felt a call to go into full-time Christian ministry. In April 2008, they officially left their comfortable and well-paid jobs to serve at Westlake Church.

When the Slacks meet people in different social settings and explain their career journey, many are perplexed. The unspoken message is why would anybody make such a rash choice? Martin and Su don't care. Their success metrics are not determined by the opinions of others. They have much higher standards.

Example 3: A Catalyst for Change with Eternal Perspective

Meet Charity Taatjes Bennett, an executive in the healthcare space and a former college classmate of mine from Taylor University. Passionate about making a difference in healthcare and impacting people's lives at their most vulnerable moments, Charity was sailing along in her career in her early 30s, securing several promotions at Priority Health. She was balancing work responsibilities with her role as a mother to three young children and wife to Derek Taatjes, who had recently transitioned away from commercial real estate to become a full-time youth pastor.

On April 14, 2011, her career and all other aspects of her life would never be the same. Charity and her two young daughters, ages two and four, were in Florida visiting her parents. Derek and the couple's six-month-old son Dylan had stayed behind in Michigan. Charity received the most devastating news that any mom or wife would ever want to hear. A fire had ignited in the family's Michigan home. The following is how Charity recapped the day on a Facebook post 10 years later:

> It was 12 AM, and my alarm was going off on my phone. My alarm was set for 12 AM to sign the girls up for swim lessons that were impossible to get into

without signing up at 12:01 on April 15th, the day they opened. I opened my computer and went to the website and signed them up for the lessons. I was awake, so I decided to check my email. There was a message with the subject line, "Are you home? Your house is on fire." Being tired and not recognizing the email address, I thought that was a horrible phishing email and deleted it.

I tried to go back to sleep but that email kept turning over in my mind, and then a clear idea, I believe from the Holy Spirit, popped into my brain— google my address. So I googled "127 Mayfield Ave Grand Rapids Michigan," and a news article showing a fire at my house popped up. I clicked into problem-solving mode. I called Derek, no answer. I called again, no answer. I called his dad, no answer. I called his mom, no answer. Everyone was asleep. I had no answers to my questions, "Was the fire really at my house?" "Were they injured? In pain?" Did I even question if they were alive? More calls to Derek, more calls to my in-laws. No answers.

I knew from the article Dylan had been taken to Helen Devos Children's Hospital and decided to call. "My name is Charity Taatjes. I am in Florida. I believe my son is at your hospital. There was a fire. He came by ambulance," I said. I was transferred, retold my story, and was transferred a few more times. Still no answers. My final transfer was to the emergency department physician who had been working on Dylan. I was given my first answer. He was gone. She had done everything she could, but my sweet baby boy that

I had only finished nursing a few weeks before was gone. Only six months of holding him, loving him and getting to know him…

I still didn't know if Derek was alive. All I knew from the article was that he was in cardiac arrest. I called my in-laws again. This time, there was an answer. My sister-in-law answered. I told her to take the phone to her dad and wake him up. I somehow got out to him what I knew. I needed him to go to the house to find out if Derek was alive. They left. I waited. Too much in shock to cry, I prayed. Confusing prayers. Please let Derek be alive. But God how would he live with knowing he had survived but Dylan had died. Would he be able to heal? But God I can't get through this loss, this pain that I know that is in front of me without Derek. This was followed by prayers without words, more groans.

My phone rang. It was my father-in-law. He told me the news. Derek was gone. They were both with Jesus. It has been inspiring to read Charity's Facebook posts over the years since this tragedy. She has always authentically communicated a resounding faith in the midst of the most crushing trial one could face. As I approached this chapter, I thought that she would be able to share with readers unique perspectives on how she approaches work since the tragedy.

After Derek and Dylan's deaths, Charity took a six-month bereavement leave to grieve her loss and adjust to a new life. She eventually decided to get back to work, motivated to return to some sort of normalcy and cognizant that she would be the sole source of income for herself and her two daughters for the foreseeable future.

87

"In an instant, I went from a pastor's wife to a widow, from having three kids to two and moving into my in-laws' basement and then to a temporary apartment," she told me. "Besides my faith, the only consistency that remained was work."

She slowly assimilated back into some semblance of a routine, while grappling with the ongoing pain from Derek and Dylan's deaths and raising two girls on her own. Charity's skills and efforts were continually noticed and appreciated over the years, resulting in a number of new roles. She is now Chief Transformation Officer at the Health Alliance Plan and the Henry Ford Health System based in Detroit.

For the most part, Charity's career goals remain similar in 2022 as they were back in her 20s prior to the tragic events she experienced. You can hear in her voice a passion to use her talents to make a difference in the healthcare space. She believes that God has called her to this work. It is also evident that her career is clearly a third priority behind God and family, which now includes her new husband George, a widower himself, and three stepchildren. Charity and George together are raising five teenage children, all of whom have experienced profound traumas in their young lives.

"I want to be a catalyst for change," Charity said. "It looks different to me all the time. It could be providing support to one of my direct reports in a 1-to-1 meeting and helping them go in the right direction. It could be providing leadership on how my organization can impact the community. It could be a conversation with my kids and husband."

While the success metrics have been constant throughout Charity's career, the perspective has evolved, particularly around how she aspires to achieve her goals and grapple with disappointments.

First, Charity believes that God has given her a platform to share her faith when the opportunity allows. She points to Kari, a colleague who was skeptical about matters of faith. Kari's interest in the gospel was piqued by attending Derek and Dylan's funeral. Upon returning to work, Charity and Kari had several conversations about Christianity and the power of the gospel message. Eventually, Kari committed her life to Christ.

Second, the tragedy has made Charity much more attune to the reality that life is precious and short, hence the importance of being intentional. This impacts how she delegates work and how she aspires to be fully present in each interaction.

"Our lives are so busy," she said. "I have to ask myself if I am spending each hour the way God called me. If we don't take time to ask that question and do this inventory, it is easy for our priorities to get away from us."

Third, Charity has a strong belief that "the greatest return on investment you can make is the time spent with other people." Through her work life and involvement with the church, Charity has poured considerable time into relationships. She saw the fruits of this investment when Derek and Dylan died, as hundreds attended the funeral and many rallied to her side in different ways. Charity was technically supposed to receive only 60 percent of her salary during her bereavement leave from work. However, a number of colleagues stepped up and donated their vacation time, thus making it possible for Charity to be compensated 100 percent during her leave.

Fourth, Charity is able to work towards her goals knowing that there will be hiccups along the way. In October 2020, Charity's role at Spectrum Health was eliminated as a result of

COVID-19. This was very painful, especially when you take into account that the 17 years she spent at the company equaled one of the few constants in her adult life that had been marked by considerable life changes. But it actually opened the door for her to assume a new senior level role at a company that provides a flexible work schedule, ideal for this season of her life.

"Losing that job really hurt," Charity shared. "But our times of affliction are literally a very brief moment compared to the glory of eternity. I learned this in losing Derek and Dylan. My joy and redemption may never be fully restored again on earth. To give an analogy, this is a tiny dot in a beautiful modern impressionistic painting of a park. All I see is the dot. God sees the beautiful picture of the park. For me, it is easier to journey through life with this perspective."

This message was reinforced during a volunteer mission trip in Kenya in which she worked with other widows. Charity concluded, "One widow said something very profound to me: 'God doesn't promise to change our circumstances. He promises to walk through them with you.'"

Zoom In on the Details of Your Career Success Picture

These three examples aren't necessarily intended to be prescriptive. You don't necessarily need to adopt each of their approaches verbatim. But hopefully, these stories provide inspiration as you consider your career success metrics. Below are two questions to get you started. You may very well come up with other related questions as you consider your own career success metrics.

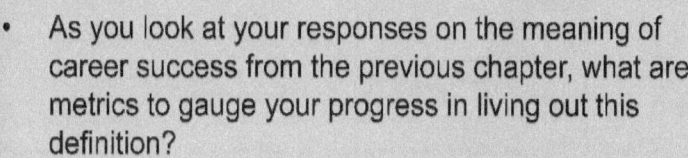

- As you look at your responses on the meaning of career success from the previous chapter, what are metrics to gauge your progress in living out this definition?

- How can you keep yourself accountable to work according to these different metrics?

PART IV

FINE-TUNING
YOUR CAREER SUCCESS
PICTURE

Principle #9: Stop Comparing

It is exciting that you have progressed to this point in answering some important questions about career success. I trust that your picture is looking clearer than when you first picked up this book. Now let's embark on some "post-production" principles.

First, we must root out comparison. Judging our work performance based on others' criteria can quickly muddle a beautiful picture of career success. Think about these questions:

- Have you ever had a bad feeling after hearing about someone's job promotion? Did it seem unfair that the person had achieved a certain title or position?
- Do you closely follow anyone on social media who drives you nuts with their humble brag posts, but for some reason you are drawn to this person's content?
- Do you ever feel bad when comparing your accomplishments to others?

I am going to guess that the overwhelming majority of people will respond "yes" to at least one of these. Count me in. Newsflash: This is terrible for us. You probably know this, even if only subconsciously. So do I. We need to be so careful about being cast under the powerful and debilitating spell of comparison and jealousy.

> Judging our work performance based on others' criteria can quickly muddle a beautiful picture of career success.

When we compare and sense that our life is better than others, it leads to pride and an unhealthy sense of superiority.

More often, we compare ourselves to others and feel that we don't measure up. That could lead us to question God.

Comparison often triggers self-pity, envy and dissatisfaction. It sucks the energy out of us. It is a waste of time that diverts us from working towards our goals. Teddy Roosevelt was indeed correct when he stated, "Comparison is the thief of joy."

Imagine being the richest man in the world yet being incredibly jealous of another person. Various public comments would seem to indicate that this was the case for Microsoft founder Bill Gates and how he saw his rival Steve Jobs of Apple, particularly throughout the 1980s and 1990s. (Reportedly, they were friendlier in later years.)

Another person who can attest to this is King Solomon, the wealthiest individual of his time. He offered a unique perspective in Ecclesiastes 4:4 when he said, "And I saw that all toil and all achievement spring from one person's envy of another. This too is meaningless, chasing after the wind." I find this verse very powerful, especially coming from someone who had it all.

Also consider the life of Saul, the first monarch of the United Kingdom of Israel. We read about his reign in the Old Testament. As the supreme ruler, Saul had everything one could imagine. Unfortunately, such prestige did not suffice. A young shepherd boy named David grew in fame for his success in battle. People began comparing David's superiority as a warrior over Saul. This does not sit well with Saul, who became inflamed with rage. Rather than using his power to advance the interests of his country, Saul got sidetracked and dedicated his time and energy to trying to kill David. He didn't succeed. Eventually, he was killed in war. He is remembered as an unsuccessful leader.

Comparison in an Online World

A *New York Times* article entitled "Don't Let Facebook Make You Miserable" highlights an interesting statistic. Americans spend about six times as much of their time cleaning dishes as they do playing golf. But there are roughly twice as many golf outing posts as there are tweets about doing the dishes.[41]

From a professional career perspective, the majority of content shared on social media is of accomplishments and expert advice. We rarely see someone post their career failures and difficult moments.

At the personal level, our social media feeds are filled with individuals' terrific vacations, happy moments and the delicious food they are about to consume. I don't see many people posting what happens behind the scenes—the day after vacation when the family returns to the stresses of their normal routines, arguments and the unappetizing food.

Outside of social media, yet still considering the realities of our digital age, we have more information than ever that can serve as a barometer to measure our own "success." We can go online to check out the real estate value of different friends and colleagues' homes, and we can make fairly educated guesses about their salaries.

With this data, we can make quick assessments about how we stack up compared to others. We can fall into the trap of pride by thinking we are better than others. Usually, though, it is the opposite. We perceive others' success to be far superior to our own, leaving us in self-pity mode.

We can also become entitled. Researchers from Swansea University and Milan University studied how social media impacts individuals' levels of narcissism, defined as entitled self-importance, and involves grandiose exhibitionism, beliefs related to entitlement and exploitation of others.

The researchers looked at the personality changes of 74 individuals aged 18 to 34 over a four-month period. The study concluded that the excessive use of social media, in particular the posting of images and selfies, is associated with a subsequent increase in narcissism.[42]

What should we do to counter these dynamics and trends? The simple solution would be to disconnect from the online world, throw away our phones and go live out in the wilderness in seclusion. But that isn't very pragmatic. While perils exist online, there are also a host of terrific ways to leverage digital technology to contribute to the betterment of our world.

We could also urge people to start posting their failures, family fights and stressful moments. But that would be counterproductive—it could lead to a sense of superiority. For years, I have been running workshops on how academics and subject matter experts can use platforms like Twitter and LinkedIn to achieve professional objectives. There is a place for transparency and making fun of oneself at times. But, by and large, I emphasize in my workshops how to share content on digital channels to align to strategic goals, including business development, networking and staying abreast of industry developments.

On the surface of it, there is nothing wrong with using social media in a strategic way as a business tool to align to our goals. You will certainly see social media content promoting various aspects of this book. The problem is when we abuse the medium.

I like to think about the positives and negatives of social media in a similar way to how we treat food. Healthy eating is terrific. A trashy diet is obviously dangerous for us.

The equivalent of healthy eating is going online for specific and strategic reasons, such as staying abreast of world news, learning the latest industry developments in your field, looking for ways to provide value to others as part of your networking strategy, identifying business development opportunities and taking part in other similar activities. It becomes unhealthy and dangerous when we get sidetracked from our purpose of being online. We can easily get cajoled into spending excessive amounts of time online, consuming or sharing content that isn't aligned to our goals. We also put ourselves in greater danger of being unproductive.

It is important to put in place guidelines to help our online activity be healthy and avoid the pitfalls of comparison. It is incumbent upon us to be aware of how we are using our time on social media and monitor reactions. Based on this, we should adapt where necessary.

There are a plethora of tools to help us be more productive and positive. They could include using timers for when you are online, removing distracting apps, adding tools that help with productivity and discussing online habits with a friend.

Comparison and Rotting Bones!

As you think about combatting comparison, keep in mind these poignant verses that highlight the dangers of comparison:

> Proverbs 14:30—"A tranquil heart gives life to the flesh, but envy makes the bones rot."

James 3:16—"For where jealousy and selfish ambition exist, there will be disorder and every vile practice." Maybe you have seen this in the workplace. I sure have. I think this is also applicable at the individual level. Does life feel properly ordered when you have negative thoughts about someone stemming from comparison? Think about how you feel inside when you hear a certain rival colleague speaking about his or her accomplishments. For me, it can make my skin crawl. I can even become angry. I would imagine that spending day and night in a state of envy would eventually make a person's bones rot metaphorically.

Recent academic research aligns to this notion. Researchers from the University of Houston and Palo Alto University conducted two studies to investigate how social comparison to peers impacts users' psychological health. In their paper, the researchers provided evidence that "people feel depressed after spending a great deal of time on Facebook because they feel bad when comparing themselves to others."[43]

We can also be encouraged to know that, when it comes to comparisons, Jesus Christ doesn't gauge our accomplishments and then decide who to love. His chosen 12 disciples weren't those of considerable status. He died for all mankind, as we covered in Principle #4. We can also counter comparison with gratitude, the topic of our next chapter.

Fine-Tuning Your Career Success Picture

As you answer the below questions, keep in mind these words of wisdom from Eleanor Roosevelt: "You wouldn't worry so much about what others think of you if you realized how seldom they do."

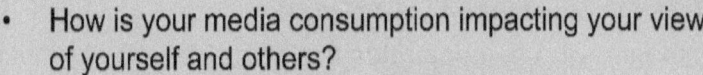

- How is your media consumption impacting your view of yourself and others?

- How much time did you spend on social media today for purposes outside of work (marketing, networking, etc.) or fulfilling a particular responsibility? Was the time spent online—whether surfing the web or perusing your social media feeds—productive and aligned to your career success definition or metrics? Were there ways that you felt more dissatisfied because, in whatever way, you were subconsciously comparing your life to others? Based on the above, how might you change the time you spend online?

- Are there safeguards you can consider implementing so that you are using your time more productively online to avoid comparison?

- How do you keep yourself grounded and humble when surrounded by successful ego-driven people?

- How can Jesus' life pragmatically help us to be content and live free from comparison?

Principle #10: Express Gratitude

While our career success picture can become distorted due to comparison, gratitude can have the opposite effect. Being grateful can help sharpen your picture.

Someone who demonstrates this characteristic of gratitude is my friend David Brühlmann, a Swiss entrepreneur now based in Cambodia, who works in the biotech consulting space and is a successful author.

David would—and should—consider himself a successful author for the incredible work he did in writing *Single for a Season: How to Be Single and Happy—A Guide for Christian Singles*. Some, however, might not consider the output a success. The book hasn't sold millions of copies. You won't find it ranked on *The New York Times* best-selling list, and he hasn't been able to sell expensive keynote speeches based on the book. In fact, David didn't achieve his ambitious goal of selling 30,000 copies when the book launched in 2021, despite putting forward his best efforts. He is able to be content and grateful, nevertheless.

"I took a huge step forward in publishing a book that I know has helped people," David said. "I still have unmet goals, but I can be content in looking at the gains. The brain tends to focus on what is lacking. We have to be deliberate in recognizing our successes as we still strive to achieve our goals."

How is it possible to have this mindset? David admits that it has been a journey and a "muscle that he has needed to develop over the years." He makes it a point to be grateful for outcomes like:

- The positive online reviews and direct feedback David received from single people who were encouraged by a book that offers an encouraging message in a society that often overlooks the well-being of single people.

- Opportunities to speak to different audiences, ranging from a church group to the biggest book publishing event in Cambodia.
- Launching a nine-week online course in Cambodia, demonstrating that a book intended for a Western audience appeals to people from different cultural and religious backgrounds.

David makes it a point to thank God each night for three things that happened in his day. This could be anything from something positive that occurred in his workday to the chance to watch a beautiful sunset.

He also believes it is important to surround himself with good people and to put himself in environments with positive energy and opportunities to be reminded of life's different

> Being grateful can help sharpen your picture.

abundances. In this respect, David has a unique advantage. In 2019, he relocated from Switzerland, one of the wealthiest countries in the world, to Cambodia. The main catalyst was to be a volunteer working on humanitarian projects. This helps with the comparison conundrum that so many of us grapple with on a regular basis.

For many of us in western developed economies, we are only seeing the successes of those who seem to be doing much better than we are. David, on the other hand, is living in a developing country and surrounded by others who are living in difficult circumstances for a myriad of different reasons that can range from education to job opportunities.

How Gratitude Provides Peace and Motivation

Hiking up a mountain is enjoyable for many. That is certainly the case for me. Being out in nature, exercising and seeing God's nature brings me great satisfaction and peace. I had the pleasure of hiking in some of the world's most beautiful mountains when I lived in Switzerland for eight years as a young adult. As a father, one of my favorite family trips was taking my wife and our boys to Utah where we hiked through canyons and mountains in stunning locations.

When you hike up a mountain, you can turn around and see how high you have climbed. You can take satisfaction in what has been accomplished. When you look ahead, you can see how much farther you need to go. You shouldn't necessarily be downtrodden because of the hike that is in front of you. Hopefully, you can approach the remaining hike with joy, appreciating the overall experience of going from the bottom to the top of the mountain.

Unfortunately, many of us—especially ambitious entrepreneurs, highly motivated creatives or hardworking professionals looking to move up the corporate ladder—don't stop to turn around and take satisfaction in the progress we have made. We fail to appreciate the challenges of the remaining journey. Instead, there is an unhealthy sense of dissatisfaction in looking up the mountain and seeing how much more progress must be made. Worse, we look at others who are already at the top and become despondent as we compare their happiness to our status quo.

We don't want to dwell on the progress that has been made in our careers for the sake of boosting our ego. But turning around every so often and recognizing the progress we have made should bring peace. When you are grateful, you tend to be happier in your outlook.

As it relates to motivation, David noted an analogy he had heard from the late American author Dale Carnegie of how two people in the same prison perceive their circumstances. One only sees the bars, but the other looks beyond the bars and sees the stars and the hope for a bright future.

10X Goals

Many people who don't hit their goals for a project only see the bars, such as feeling the frustration of not hitting a sales target. David is like the other prisoner who sees the opportunities ahead. This outlook gives David the permission to set 10x goals. These are goals that are 10 times greater than the actual objective you had in mind. According to David, they free you up for wild and creative thinking. It was interesting for me to hear this perspective, as I have always looked to establish goals that are very conservative so that I can increase the likelihood of achieving them, thus not setting myself up for disappointment if I don't meet the goal.

Neither the 10x or conservative approach in goal setting is right or wrong, per se. But it is interesting to see how gratitude closely connects to having the freedom to go for big audacious goals outside our comfort zones. Even if the goal isn't achieved, gratefulness for what has been accomplished can keep a person pressing forward and avoiding the pitfalls of complacency.

"I maintain focus on the goal but don't let it dictate my state of happiness," David said. "I find happiness in the progress I have made. I set big goals but am also realistic. The chances of any author making *The New York Times* best seller list are small. The number of copies sold is not the only metric for success. More important are the lives that can be changed."

Research

Imagine spending a day focusing only on things that aggravate you. Contemplate every aspect of life that is wrong. Dwell on goals unachieved. How would you feel at the end of that day?

Now, imagine the opposite scenario. Focus solely on the positive aspects of your life. Dwell on the achievements—large or small—that happened today. How do you think you will feel at the end of the day?

I think you know the answer to the two different scenarios posed here. But, in case you have any doubt, consider gratitude research conducted by Dr. Robert A. Emmons of the University of California, Davis, and Dr. Michael E. McCullough of the University of Miami.

In one study, Emmons and McCullough had a group of participants write a few sentences each week, focusing on particular topics. One group wrote about what they were grateful for from the past week. The other group wrote about irritations or things that had bothered them. A third group wrote about events that had affected them but didn't emphasize whether the events were positive or negative. After 10 weeks, the group that wrote about what they were grateful for expressed more optimism and felt better about their lives. They exercised more frequently and had fewer visits to physicians compared to the group that wrote about their aggravations.[44]

This research really shouldn't come as a surprise, right? Yet, if you were to reflect on your own conversations, what is the breakdown between gratitude and cynicism? As you think about your thoughts, how often do you contemplate what you want to achieve versus expressing gratitude for what you have accomplished to date. If you eavesdrop on a conversation at a coffee shop, how often do you hear people expressing genuine appreciation for life as opposed to griping about what is wrong? When you peruse your social media feeds, what percentage of the content skews towards gratitude compared to the posts and comments that are contrary to this?

The Power of Rejoicing

Consider the power of contentment and gratitude according to the Bible.

Philippians 4:4

"Rejoice in the Lord always. I will say it again: Rejoice!"

Note that Paul wrote this while he was unjustly imprisoned for simply preaching the gospel of Jesus Christ.

1 Thessalonians 5:16–18

"Rejoice always, pray continually, give thanks in all circumstances; for this is God's will for you in Christ Jesus."

Here, Paul again implores us to find satisfaction not just when life is going according to our plans but in all circumstances.

Psalm 118:24

"This is the day that the Lord has made; let us rejoice and be glad in it."

Note that it doesn't say we should rejoice if the days are sunny and successful. "This" would imply to each and every day.

Practices to Consider

These verses provide clear guidance on how to rejoice in both good and bad times at work. There are several implications related to gratitude. Here are three daily practices to consider:

1. Thank God Daily

Each night, thank God for at least three positive things that happened in your day. Whether it is something significant or a minor detail that we might overlook, thanking God daily for the positive aspects of your life will provide many benefits for the soul. This gratefulness forces you to recognize the positive aspects of your life that you might otherwise overlook. It also can help anchor you to the reality that God is in control of all the circumstances of your life.

2. Keep the Right Company

Be careful of the company that you keep. It is amazing how positive people can help give us energy and put a smile on our faces, while the words and wisdom of pessimistic complainers can sour our mood.

Of course, there are some instances when we have to be around people who aren't the positive uplifters. We can't always avoid certain colleagues or family members. In these instances, it is important to be on guard. Realize in advance that you may be entering a negative environment and be prepared not to let that person's energy impact your mood.

Better yet, consider how you can respond to the negativity with encouragement and, thus, be the spark that ignites positive energy in others.

I also think it is important to not be so engulfed with our niche industry that we fail to hear outside perspectives. If you are a marketer working in the pharmaceutical industry, and most of your time is spent with people working in that profession and/or industry, your perspectives will tend to be skewed towards only what is important to the consensus of that group. Now, imagine you are a marketer working in the pharmaceutical industry, and you have a range of interesting outside hobbies and interests. You spend considerable time volunteering and learn new skills outside of marketing and the pharmaceutical industry. I think in this scenario, you are more likely to see other ways of living and have exposure to new people than you are accustomed to and, thus, will be in a better place to experience gratitude for your life.

3. Seek Support

Find a friend or community group that integrates to some extent the principle of gratitude. David and I meet weekly to support each other's business goals and keep one another accountable. These Zoom sessions are a source of inspiration. In part, we put emphasis on recognizing accomplishments before delving into addressing challenges for the week. I have also been a part of mastermind groups that included four to six people and provided the same venue for sharing successes and encouragement.

I understand that scheduling a regular call with such an individual or group can be more complicated for people working a full-time role as opposed to an entrepreneur who might have more independence over his or her schedule. Don't let that stop you. Hopefully, your colleagues can appreciate that networking and knowledge sharing is a powerful way to grow individually and that you can bring such learning and growth to your role. If there are doubts, communicate this message. If it is not well received, then be creative and find times outside the normal workday. It will be time incredibly well spent. Many of us are isolated enough as it is. We are not intended to be growing in our careers on our own desert islands. Community is critical.

It can also be a challenge to find the right group for various reasons. Perhaps the initial person or group you try doesn't seem to be a good connection. I encourage you to approach such meetings with an open mind. It is fine if those in your group are at different points in their career or work in industries completely different to the one you are in. Fresh and new perspectives from an outsider can often go a long way to supporting you.

If the group just doesn't seem to be the right fit—whether due to the personalities present or the format—and you are not leaving the meetings with more gratitude in your heart, then there is nothing wrong with diplomatically cutting ties and finding a group or partner that is a better fit.

Fine-Tuning Your Career Success Picture

Here are some questions and points to consider (ideally to discuss with a friend or in a small group).

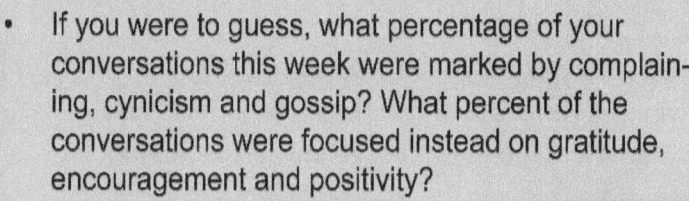

- If you were to guess, what percentage of your conversations this week were marked by complaining, cynicism and gossip? What percent of the conversations were focused instead on gratitude, encouragement and positivity?

- In what ways should you be looking to make changes with the company you keep?

- Do you have a friend, accountability partner, mentor, career coach or mastermind group that can help you live out your definition of career success and do so with gratitude?

Principle #11: Pray with Perspective

Another critical component to sharpening or potentially adjusting your career success definition is prayer.

Based on what I have learned over the years from so many resources, prayer is about connecting and building a relationship with God. It entails listening, meditating, seeking forgiveness and worshiping an all-powerful higher being. Career-related prayers can tend to solely focus on satisfying earthly ambitions that advance our own interests. I certainly have been guilty of this in the past.

> Prayer is about connecting and building a relationship with God.

Tim Keller, in a sermon entitled "Jesus' Prayer for All Time," says, "There are people who basically just use prayer as a way of getting power, and then there are people who use prayer to get to know and be with God."[45]

Consider research from Harvard that investigated the effects of prayer on patients undergoing coronary artery bypass surgery. Some 1,800 participants were divided into three groups of about 600 each. One group received no prayers. A second group received prayers after being told that they may or may not be prayed for. Members of the third group were informed that others would pray for them for 14 straight days. The prayers came from various Christian groups. Results showed that the individuals' prayers didn't have an impact. Here were some of the results:[46]

- There were 197 cardiac complications among the group that knew outsiders were praying for them compared with 187 and 158 in the other two groups.
- Complications occurred in 59 percent of those who were prayed for compared with 51 percent of those who received no prayers.
- The number of deaths during the 30 days after surgery was similar across the groups.

This study demonstrates an important point related to how we should pray about our career issues and pitfalls to avoid. From afar, it seems like participants in this study took the "vending machine" approach to prayer. This is the prevalent mindset that if we say the right words in a prayer, God owes us what we request, just like putting a couple bucks in the vending machine means we are owed the candy bar of our choice. This approach to prayer sets us up for disappointments.

It is worth noting the challenges of measuring the impact of something as intimate and personal as prayer. I am sure that, coming out of Harvard, the above research is thorough and comprehensive. But the way this study was carried out feels very much like the vending machine approach to prayer. I am going to make an educated guess that the participants in the study were motivated to pray in large part due to the pressure of committing to the study, as opposed to building a relationship to God. It also runs counterintuitive to the personal nature of prayer in which we freely communicate to God rather than being cajoled into doing so.

Part of prayer does indeed entail that we ask God to supply our daily needs. But that is just one part of it. The words uttered in a prayer shouldn't be posed as demands that God owes us in some way but, rather, requests submitted in humbleness. For the record, I do believe that God does miracles and intervenes on behalf of people's prayers. But we should be careful in our approach and expectations. When praying, we need to ensure that requests are submitted to his will. God knows best, and he doesn't always answer our prayers the way we express them.

Throughout the history of mankind, millions of people have lain on their deathbeds while friends and family expressed prayers for healing and survival. From the start of mankind until the end of the 19th century, every person in this predicament died, even Jesus (though he exceptionally rose again). The same will be true for many of us reading this book who will be on our deathbeds one day.

As it relates to praying about work, we might subconsciously believe that if we pray long and hard enough, God will grant us the desired promotion or achievement. We can become disheartened when these efforts go unanswered. We also miss the entire point of the practice and the other benefits that come from it that give us true peace and motivation. When we treat prayer like a genie that grants us our wishes, it becomes difficult to build the connection that is possible with God.

While the research doesn't support immediate answers to prayers, it is interesting that there are studies supporting the notion of prayer providing a sense of peace. Tyler VanderWeele, a Harvard professor, led a study that found that young adults who prayed daily tended to have fewer depressive symptoms in comparison to those who never prayed.[47] The praying people also had higher levels of life satisfaction, self-esteem and positivity. I can certainly attest to these types of outcomes as well.

"Pre-joicing"

I heard a fantastic example of the opposite to the vending machine approach while listening to Jordan Raynor's terrific podcast, *Called to Mastery*. Jordan's guest was Valerie Woerner, founder of Val Marie Paper. Val was coming out with her new book in October 2021 called *Pray Confidently and Consistently*. It was a project two years in the making. As you might guess from the topic of the book, Val was regularly praying for the book project, even fasting one time per week as the launch date drew near. She explained on the podcast:

> The Tuesday before the book came out, I decided to start feasting, and basically, I decided to "pre-joice." This is a term I write about in my book that basically means rejoicing before what we are asking God for actually happens. It is a statement of faith and celebration.
>
> My joy wasn't determined by launch day, and thank God it wasn't. My book actually ended up not being in stores at all, and I didn't find out until the day before. It was a crushing blow. I am so thankful that I had the Tuesday before to have such a sweet day of celebration. Launch day was very different than expected, and I am thankful that I was able to enjoy that without having circumstances determine it.[48]

Note that Val wasn't thanking God in advance for achieving her success metrics! She was thanking God whether those goals were met or not.

"Nothing should steal the joy of working for two years on a book and knowing that you are proud of it and God was working throughout," she added. "That was my way of not waiting for permission from other people to rejoice in the work.

But you have to do this before you hear the noise from the world."

Prayer Frameworks for Perspective

There have been many ups and downs in my prayer life over the years. That confession out of the way, there are three different types of prayer formats that have worked very well for me in praying about career disappointments and aspirations.

The Lord's Prayer

First, Jesus gives us a great framework with the Lord's Prayer. This was the prayer that Jesus recommended to the multitudes in attendance for the famous Sermon on the Mount recorded in Matthew 6.

Many people—Christians and non-Christians alike—can recite the Lord's Prayer from memory. When something is quite popular, however, the words can lose their meaning. For so long, the Lord's Prayer really didn't mean much to me until I listened to a sermon series preached by Randy Pope of Perimeter Church in Georgia. Over the course of several weeks, Pope dedicated an entire series to just a few of the words from the Lord's Prayer. If you want to hear it for yourself, I encourage you to check out this series.[49]

One of the things that I really like about the Lord's prayer is the order. It helps to keep things in perspective. We start by recognizing God as our Father. We then segue to focusing on his great attributes by hallowing his name or recognizing his holiness. It continues with a prayer for God's will to be done on earth as in heaven and then seeking forgiveness. God does want to hear our specific requests, and so we are encouraged to ask him to give us our daily bread. It feels like a natural order that keeps things in good perspective.

The sermon series taught me the importance of personalizing the Lord's Prayer as opposed to simply reciting it. So, I will take the different words that Jesus shared as a model and then make it applicable to my own life. For example, when I say, "Our Father," I find it useful to meditate upon what it means to have a God who acts as our loving father, treating us as his special children. For "give us this day our daily bread," I will pray for specific requests related to my work, family and other activities. I apply such personalization for each phrase of the Lord's Prayer.

ACTS

Another framework that works well for me is the ACTS acronym that is a model for prayer taught by many. It stands for:

A—Adoration (expressing praise to God)

C—Confession (seeking forgiveness)

T—Thanksgiving (gratitude)

S—Supplication (making our requests known to God)

Career Success Definition

Sometimes, I pray over my career success definition. It sounds like a combination of statements of affirmation and a prayer. When we discussed Principle #7, I noted that one of my career success bullet points is, "I am a child of God. I will do my work with integrity." As I walk around my neighborhood, I will pray something to the effect of, "I am a child God. Dear God, help me to display integrity today through my decisions and in my interactions with others."

115

Frameworks like these three keep me disciplined and praying regularly. They prompt me to be holistic, encourage connection to God and help me to avoid the vending machine approach.

There are obviously many other ways to pray and connect to God. Each person's prayer life will look different, as should be the case, considering the personal nature of interacting with God. There can be great impact in meditating on different passages from the Bible. Some people experience connection with God through fasting. There is power in praying in community. There are many other dimensions to prayer—refer to the Holy Bible for more insights on this!

Fine-Tune Your Career Success Picture

Here are some questions and points to consider (ideally to discuss with a friend or in a small group).

- Do you pray for your career-related matters? If yes, how has it helped you in the past? In what ways have you been disappointed by unanswered career-related prayers?

- Are there ways for you to apply the idea of "pre-joicing" as described by Valerie?

- What are actions that you can take to connect with God while praying for career-related matters?

Principle #12: Discover Growth and New Direction

What should you do in the face of disappointments and letdowns? If you don't feel like your current circumstances are aligned to your career success definition, should you pivot and change course in some dramatic way? Or do you view this as an opportunity for growth? Addressing these questions is a final post-production component to consider about your career success picture.

Persevering

In August 2021, I attended the virtual Global Leadership Summit event and heard the inspiring story of Jamie Kern Lima, an American entrepreneur, investor and media personality. In 2008, she launched a company called IT Cosmetics to provide makeup products to women like herself who struggled with a particular skin condition.

A terrific orator, Jamie shared all the struggles and rejections that she had experienced over the years. A number of beauty retailers rejected her products. She even joked that when her company launched a new product line and registered a sale, she was initially ecstatic. That is until she realized it wasn't from a real customer. Rather, it was her husband, the company's website designer, testing the user experience.

Still, Jamie kept the faith in her company and in God. At the Global Leadership Summit, she repeated a refrain several times, "Do we listen to the *no* or the *knowing*?" The "knowing" in this case is God. Eventually, her prayers were answered.

She was featured on a 10-minute QVC segment that led to her product selling out. She became a regular on QVC, and her company was eventually acquired by L'Oréal for $1.2 billion in 2016.[50]

This is a lovely story. It would make for a great Hollywood movie. Perseverance is a great characteristic. So, too, is trusting in God. If we follow Jamie's example, we need to be careful about expecting similar fame and fortune. Sometimes, the "no" might actually be the answer that we must accept.

Pivoting

For every Jamie Kern Lima, there are also people who must respond to the disappointment differently and pivot.

Take for example Kelsey Kemp, an ex-tech consultant turned career coach. Her disappointment: She had been unable to fulfill a dream to move from Texas and continue her career as a tech consultant in London, UK. Coincidentally, one day while scrolling through *The Muse* (a blog devoted to career development), she stumbled upon someone with her exact same name. The Kelsey featured in the article had also wanted to move to London and discover her calling. However, she ultimately realized that she was just trying to escape her life. Some weeks later, Kelsey Kemp found the podcast of the Kelsey featured in that *Muse* article and listened to an interview in which the guest—who, funnily enough, was also named Kelsey (yes, a third Kelsey)—spoke about being a career coach.

Kelsey Kemp believes that the Lord showed her through this series of events that she was to no longer fixate on the consulting career in London but, rather, pivot. She promptly signed up for a coaching certification course and then ultimately started her new company.

Then, there is Deborah Osomo. Born in Nigeria, Deborah set out for Texas in 2013 and graduated from LeTourneau University four years later with a degree in early childhood education. She then decided to pursue a master's degree at New York University with the goal of graduating, publishing her research in high-profile journals and eventually working for a prestigious international education organization tied to the United Nations.

These were all very nice goals that were completely upended when the COVID-19 pandemic shut down most everything, including universities like NYU. Deborah returned to her home city of Abuja, Nigeria, with the goal to work. She planned to make money so she could continue her education at NYU once the pandemic ended. This plan too was derailed due to administrative bureaucracy. The paperwork she needed never went through, and Deborah couldn't legally work as a public servant within the country.

With more time on her hands than normal, Deborah began creating YouTube videos focused on career development tips for teachers. To her surprise, many teachers began to provide feedback. They really liked the content.

Deborah then rolled out some paid services and soon realized that she had a viable business. These circumstances led her to a pivot, culminating with the launch of her own coaching company for teachers called The Purposeful Educator. Deborah believes that she can have more of an impact with this company than if she had pursued her initial goal of working within the UN system.

"This taught me what it means to totally surrender to God's plans," said Deborah. "We can't always see what God has in store for us when he closes one door. Maybe another door will open; maybe not. We can be at peace that other possibilities await when we have a mindset of surrendering to these plans. It is not always easy, and it's a journey."

Another person who saw a setback as an opportunity to pivot is Michael Hyatt, a former executive with Thomas Nelson Publishing. Back in 2003, Michael slipped and fell while running out of the house to get to work on time, as he described on the Full Focus website.[51] The result was a broken ankle. Michael had to put a pause on his many leadership demands.

Stuck in bed, Michael used the down time to discover the practicality of blogging. This would be a catalyst for him to eventually leave Thomas Nelson Publishing some years later and launch a new business called Michael Hyatt and Company (eventually renamed to Full Focus). The leadership development firm has helped countless individuals through its content, courses, coaching services and events.

This book you are reading is the result of a career disruption. I am currently writing this chapter in February 2022 from a hotel room in Dubai. I was supposed to be here for three days for a client event taking place at the World Expo. My event concluded on a Friday afternoon, and I happily dashed off for some sight-seeing activities. I was planning to buy some gifts for my wife and sons before flying back home to Florida the following morning. I then received a text message noting that I was COVID-19 positive, despite having no symptoms, and that I needed to quarantine for 7–10 days.

Initially, it was overwhelming to figure out the protocols I needed to adhere to in a country far from home. Florida's approach to dealing with positive COVID-19 cases is diametrically opposed to that of the United Arab Emirates. It was overwhelming to think about being confined to a random hotel room out in the middle of nowhere. But, on the first full day of my quarantine, I heard on a podcast that JK Rowling would spend her own money to stay in a nice hotel in order to gain the clarity to write her books.[52] It dawned on me that these circumstances provided me with an opportunity to hone in on the content for this book during my 10-day quarantine period.

Discerning

As we face disappointments in our careers, we have to choose one of the following:

a) Is this a door closing? Do we need to reverse course?

b) Is this just a temporary roadblock? Do we need to persist to reach our goal?

c) Is this a combination of the above? Should we continue persisting at one goal while exploring other avenues?

Answer: Sometimes, the correct answer is a, b or c. I know that isn't entirely helpful. All the different examples presented here purposely show one of these three scenarios playing out.

Unfortunately, I can't articulate a six-step process to follow that will guarantee you answers and clarity. It would be great if there were always a crystal-clear answer. In addition, there is never one single way to find out what the answer is. It will vary depending on the person and the situation. God directs us in various ways.

Sometimes, the directional nudge can seem obvious. In the case of Kelsey Kemp, she clearly interpreted God's direction from the random content she consumed that specifically correlated to her dilemma over moving to London. In the case of Deborah, there wasn't a clear answer, but different circumstances necessitated a new path.

Following are several points to consider and tactics to deploy to help move you along.

1. Pray

While the previous chapter is dedicated to the topic of prayer, I would be remiss if I didn't mention that prayer should play a leading role in helping us discern God's calling. Note some of the caveats explained in the remainder of this section and the previous one.

2. Know We Have a Choice

In all the examples, the individuals involved had some degree of choice. Tim Keller, in a sermon preached at Redeemer Presbyterian Church in 2004, uses a terrific example to illustrate this. He asks congregants to imagine a 20-year-old college student calling up his father to ask for permission to go outside and play frisbee with friends. The father would say, "What is wrong with you? I don't know. You know your workload. You can make these decisions by yourself."[53]

In the same sermon, Keller points out that he was never 100 percent sure and at peace that he had been called by God to move from rural Virginia to start a church in New York City. He says:

I can be absolutely sure I mustn't lie—it is in the Bible. I can be sure I mustn't bow down to idols—it is in the Bible. I am sure of a lot of things that are God's will. But as far as I know, I won't be sure I was called to plant a new church until it happens. Then I will know. Guidance is as much as something God does as something God gives.

All this illustrates that there isn't a one-size-fits-all answer to this question of whether to persevere or pivot.

3. Change Your Outlook

It is always useful to consider the past—to some extent. Looking back and thinking through different situations allows us to glean important lessons. But, spending too much time dwelling on events that are out of our control is usually counterproductive. It would be a far better investment of time to think about the steps to take moving forward.

In a blog post entitled "A Question that Changes Everything," Michael Hyatt, whose story I highlighted earlier, wrote, "One of the best questions you can ask when something negative happens is this: 'What does this experience make possible?' Do you see the subtle shift? Suddenly, your attention moves from the past—which you can't do a thing about—to the future."[54]

I encourage you to consider this question next time you face a career roadblock. Find a trusted friend whom you can discuss this matter with and brainstorm ideas. I trust that it will change your mindset in the positive direction.

As part of your outlook, think also about using whatever period of uncertainty to consider your priorities, as we delved into when we discussed Principle #7. Are your priorities for your other identities in balance? Is it possible you are too fixated on whatever career dilemma you are encountering at the expense of faith, family, friends and community?

4. Seek Out People to Give You Wise Counsel

Stumped by the lack of growth of my Global Innovators Academy project, I decided to hire an outside coach to provide perspective. I called upon someone whose judgment and acumen I admired from afar—Mark Schaefer, a well-known blogger, author and consultant in the marketing space. During our coaching call, I outlined my journey and vision for the project with great passion and excitement. I was hopeful that Mark would share some of his marketing genius that I could then apply to my situation.

After about 20 minutes of questions and answers, Mark provided his guidance. It wasn't what I wanted to hear. He basically told me that he didn't see a viable pathway for me to grow this initiative to the levels I had aspired to in its current format. He didn't slam the door shut on the project, though, noting that there were valuable ways the program could make a difference in refugees, one of the student populations I'd had the opportunity to work with earlier that year.

Still, it was quite a blow. I concluded the call and moped around for the next day. But, it was exactly what I had needed to hear. Other than a few online exchanges, I hadn't met Mark before. That was a huge advantage in proceeding with the call, as Mark could be direct with me.

In response to the question of pivoting or persevering, the conversation with Mark led me to answer letter C—tweak my program and don't give up on it, but also consider other projects to pursue. This coaching call played a role in leading me to write this book while continuing to do my ongoing communications consulting work, which has been the bread and butter of my business since 2013.

The lesson from my coaching call with Mark is that we all need to find friends, colleagues and maybe even trusted experts who we don't know well to give us honest feedback. The keyword is *honest*. Encouragement and rah rah support does have its place. But, cheering someone on a journey into a ditch isn't very good encouragement.

5. Have Patience!

In early 2022, I was part of a weekly Zoom call as part of a group called Faith Driven Entrepreneur. Six other business owners and I met to connect, support and grow through various activities. In one of the calls, Mark Sherman, owner of a digital marketing firm, shared about the

> Remember that it took 33 years before Jesus Christ was called to bring about the pinnacle moment of his "career" on earth.

long time it took for him to get the business where he wanted. It is far from the indirect "get rich quick messages" we frequently hear about. He said he didn't really achieve his goals for about 18 years!

In the Bible, we frequently read stories about pivots and perseverance. They usually don't happen overnight. Think about Joseph in the Old Testament. He spent years in difficult circumstances as a slave and then a prisoner before he was appointed by Pharoah to be in charge of the whole land of Egypt (essentially the number two in government).

Remember that it took 33 years before Jesus was called to bring about the pinnacle moment of his "career" on earth.

Fine-Tune Your Career Success Picture

Here are some questions and points to consider (ideally to discuss with a friend or in a small group).

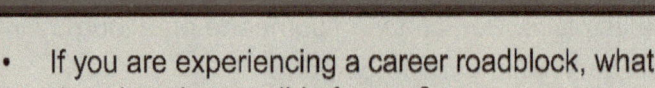

- If you are experiencing a career roadblock, what does it make possible for you?

- How might God be working through your career circumstances to help you identify new opportunities?

- Do you have a trusted friend or mentor that you can reach out to who can provide truly honest and open feedback with your best interests in mind? If not, what steps can you take to identify such an individual?

- What are new actions that you can take to gain clarity?

- How might answers to the above questions shape any tweaks you make to your career success definition and the related metrics?

PART V

MAKE IT VISIBLE

Conclusion

If you have made it this far, give yourself a pat on the back! You have zoomed out on the external factors that underscore how God is in control in the midst of our professional ups and downs. You have considered the different angles to avoid that can cause distortion in determining what career success entails. You have zoomed in on what career success means for you and have considered ways to fine-tune this picture. Among other things, getting to this point signals that you are thinking deeply about what career success means for you from various vantage points.

Here is my next challenge for you. Please make some of your responses to the key questions in this book visible to yourself in some way. We hang up memorable pictures on the walls of our homes or offices for various reasons. A framed picture on the wall of a family vacation serves as a fun memory. In the same way, a picture of a quote or saying can serve as a reminder, inspiration or call to action.

If you have taken the time to think through the important questions in this book—especially the definition of career success and the related metrics—please make this visible to yourself in whatever way works best for you. It is my hope that your visible reminder will serve as an ongoing source of peace and motivation and also a guide for decision-making.

If you journal, you could write out your responses and refer to them regularly. You could also have these responses in a prominent place on your computer, such as a screensaver or desktop wallpaper. If you use an organizing software, such as Evernote or Notion, you could feature your answers in prominent places within these tools.

I also want to encourage you to literally frame a picture of some of your key answers and keep them visible at your place of work. You could design something on your own and place it in a small frame for your desk or some other prominent location.

> It is my hope that your visible reminder will serve as an ongoing source of peace and motivation and also a guide for decision-making.

If you see the importance of framing your answers but don't have the time or energy to create something on your own, then you can use some of the design options available at www.reframingcareersuccess.com/frames.

In addition, many of the questions posed in this book are topics that we should be reflecting on regularly throughout our careers. I want to help you do this and also learn from you. Receive updates and encouragement about how the gospel message can help us be content and motivated in the midst of professional highs and lows. Join our community by signing up at www.reframingcareersuccess.com.

I welcome the opportunity to connect with you individually. Feel free to email me at kevin.anselmo@gmail.com. Thank you so much for reading this book and joining me on this journey to reframe career success!

NOTES

Acknowledgements

Only one individual's name is highlighted as the author of this book. However, a number of people have helped make this final version possible.

First, I need to recognize my immediate family. My wife Nicole has been a big supporter of this project. I am grateful for both her editorial feedback and encouragement. An interesting turning point for this book came in dialogue with my two sons, ages 8 and 10. While trying to impart life wisdom on how to manage one's homework load, I decided to share my own challenges in writing a book, which can also feel quite overwhelming. What I thought would be a passing reference instead turned into a barrage of questions about my book. Both of my sons shared a deep interest in my work, more so than any work project I might have mentioned in the past. In fact, both have taken the time to read parts of the book with me and offered me encouragement. This has been very touching to me.

I would like to recognize my parents, Paul and Diana Anselmo. From an early age, I was fortunate to learn from parental figures who brought a faith-based approach to their various work activities.

I want to thank every person who shared their story with me in an interview. This book wouldn't be what it is without their stories and the insights they were willing to share.

There are two individuals who I never really met in person, yet their insights have helped shape my thinking about faith and work. First is Timothy Keller, founding pastor of Redeemer Presbyterian Church and author of many terrific Christian books. Keller's insights about the gospel message have impacted my life tremendously. I am also grateful to Jordan Raynor. His books and podcasts have also played a very helpful role in how I view faith and work topics.

Thanks so much to Dr. Alan Wilson, who did a comprehensive theological review of this book for me. I am grateful for his challenging questions that prompted me to re-write and improve various sections.

Elizabeth Hunter was a terrific copyeditor, pointing out typos and challenging me to delve deeper on certain topics. Sara Pack provided exceptional proofreading and book formatting support.

David Brühlmann also has played an important role in bringing this book to fruition. David and I meet on a regular basis to provide each other with encouragement and offer advice on our different entrepreneurial ventures. I was inspired by David's approach to writing his book, *Single for a Season*. Our conversations played a role in bringing me to write this book.

I am grateful to Janet Shaner, Ashley Taylor, Mark Sherman, Nuno Fernandes, Bob Durbois and Adam Khorshid for reading drafts of this book and providing terrific feedback. Svitlana Stefaniuk provided invaluable support in designing the book cover and brand attributes. You can learn more about her work at https://www.bringyou.art/.

Also, I would like to recognize my launch team! I certainly don't have the platform and marketing budget to ensure that this book is read by as many as the Lord wills. I appreciate each individual who shared a social media post and recommended the book to a friend.

Finally and most importantly, I have to thank the Good Lord! It would only be fitting that a book on faith and work conclude with such an acknowledgement. Thank you, God, for using my gifts and shortcomings to write such a book!

Partners

Veth Group are experts at helping you book meetings with your target business buyers, using email, direct mail and LinkedIn. We are grateful to the Veth Group for partnering with us on running a campaign for *Reframing Career Success*. Learn more at vethgroup.com.

NEH Media is a digital marketing agency. NEH Media provides strategic, data-driven, holistic and ethical coaching to improve organizations' visibility, increase their traffic, and grow their business. We are grateful to NEH Media for partnering with us on various aspects of marketing *Reframing Career Success*. Learn more at nehmedia.com.

References

Introduction
1. Thompson, Karl. "What Percentage of Your Life Will You Spend at Work?" Revise Sociology, August 16, 2016, https://revisesociology.com/2016/08/16/percentage-life-work/.

Principle #1
2. https://hymnary.org/text/when_peace_like_a_river_attendeth_my_way.

3. https://en.wikipedia.org/wiki/Great_Chicago_Fire.

4. David Anspaugh, director, *Rudy*. TriStar Pictures, 1993.

5. Raj Raghunathan, "Why Losing Control Can Make You Happier," *Greater Good Magazine*, September 28, 2016, https://greatergood.berkeley.edu/article/item/why_losing_control_make_you_happier.

Principle #2
6. Clint Eastwood, director, *Invictus*. Spyglass Entertainment, 2009.

7. https://poets.org/poem/invictus.

8. Jim Harter, "U.S. Employee Engagement Drops for First Year in a Decade," Gallup, https://www.gallup.com/workplace/388481/employee-engagement-drops-first-year-decade.aspx.

9. Alex Trebek, *The Answer Is . . .: Reflections on My Life*, Simon & Schuster, 2020.

10. https://en.wikipedia.org/wiki/Emily_Dickinson.

11. Klaus Issler, "Jesus's Career…Before His Ministry," Institute for Faith, Work and Economics, May 7, 2014, https://tifwe.org/jesus-career-before-his-ministry/.

Principle #3

12. https://m.imdb.com/name/nm0000226/quotes.

13. Russell E. Johnson, Stanley B. Silverman, Aarti Shyamsunder, Hsien-Yao Swee, O. Burcu Rodopman, Eunae Cho & Jeremy Bauer, "Acting Superior But Actually Inferior?: Correlates and Consequences of Workplace Arrogance," *Human Performance*, 23:5, 403–427, https://doi.org/10.1080/08959285.2010.515279.

14. 2021 NBA Finals Press Conference, July 20, 2021, https://www.youtube.com/watch?v=HwO52X1Pg_c.

15. Jason Hehir, director, *The Last Dance*. ESPN Films. 2020.

16. https://quotefancy.com/quote/1253477/Phil-Jackson-You-re-only-a-success-for-the-moment-that-you-complete-a-successful-act.

17. Curtis "50 Cent" Jackson, *Hustle Harder, Hustle Smarter*, HarperCollins Publishers, 2021.

18. Psychology Today Staff, "The Hedonic Treadmill," *Psychology Today*, https://www.psychologytoday.com/us/basics/hedonic-treadmill.

19. Mike Cosper, host, "The Rise and Fall of Mars Hill," *Christianity Today*, 2021, https://www.christianitytoday.com/ct/podcasts/rise-and-fall-of-mars-hill/.

20. Michael E. Porter and Nitin Nohria, "How CEOs Manage Time," *Harvard Business Review*, July–August 2018, https://hbr.org/2018/07/how-ceos-manage-time.

21. Rhymer Rigby, "Good chiefs look after their family and spouse," *The Financial Times*, April 29, 2015, https://www.ft.com/content/345e4a9c-e759-11e4-8e3f-00144feab7de.

22. Pew Research Center, "Being Christian in Western Europe," May 29, 2018, https://www.pewforum.org/2018/05/29/being-christian-in-western-europe/.

23. Philip Jenkins, "How Africa Is Changing Faith Around the World," July 5, 2016, https://www.pewtrusts.org/en/trend/archive/summer-2016/how-africa-is-changing-faith-around-the-world.

24. John Flavel, "Keeping the Heart," Preach the Word, https://www.preachtheword.com/bookstore/keepingheart.pdf

25. Press Conferences after the 2022 Masters, April 10, 2022, https://www.youtube.com/watch?v=EsGakPD0-Yo.

Principle #5

26. Oracle Press Release, "82% of People Believe Robots Can Support Their Career Better Than Humans," October 26, 2021, https://www.oracle.com/news/announcement/people-believe-robots-can-support-their-career-2021-10-26/.

27. William A. Kahn, "Psychological Conditions of Personal Engagement and Disengagement at Work," *Academy of Management Journal*, Vol. 33, No. 4 Articles, Published online November 30, 2017, https://doi.org/10.5465/256287.

Principle #6

28. Richard Stearns, *Lead Like It Matters to God*, InterVarsity Press, 2021, https://www.ivpress.com/lead-like-it-matters-to-god.

29. Derek Thompson, "Workism Is Making Americans Miserable," *The Atlantic*, February 24, 2019, https://www.theatlantic.com/ideas/archive/2019/02/religion-workism-making-americans-miserable/583441/.

30. David Brooks, *The Road to Character*, Random House Publishers, 2016, https://theroadtocharacter.com.

31. R. Paul Stevens lecture, "The Spirituality of Work," Center for Faith + Work Los Angeles, October 3, 2018, https://www.youtube.com/watch?v=NmWRToGR2Kw.

32. Paige Leskin, "American kids want to be famous on YouTube, and kids in China want to go to space: survey," *Business Insider*, July 17, 2019. https://www.businessinsider.com/american-kids-youtube-star-astronauts-survey-2019-7.

33. https://mediakix.com/blog/percent-children-becoming-a-youtuber/.

34. Stéphane Garelli, "Why you will probably live longer than most big companies," IMD Business School, December 2016, https://www.imd.org/research-knowledge/articles/why-you-will-probably-live-longer-than-most-big-companies/.

35. https://en.wikipedia.org/wiki/Cornelius_Vanderbilt.

Principle #7

36. Dieudonné Tamfu, "The Gods of the Prosperity Gospel," Desiring God, February 4, 2020, https://www.desiringgod.org/articles/the-gods-of-the-prosperity-gospel.

37. Daniel Boerman, "Is Prosperity a Blessing?" *The Banner*, January 18, 2011, https://www.thebanner.org/features/2011/01/is-prosperity-a-blessing.

38. Vaneetha Rendall Risner, "What Does It Really Mean to Be #Blessed?" Desiring God, April 28, 2016, https://www.desiringgod.org/articles/what-does-it-really-mean-to-be-blessed.

39. Forbes Staff, "The Gods of the Prosperity Gospel," September 14, 2001, https://www.forbes.com/2001/09/14/0914ladenmoney.html?sh=7d6a4cec32a3.

40. Mary Hanbury and Áine Cain, "No one knows Putin's exact net worth, but many speculate he's the wealthiest person on the planet—his $1 billion palace and $500 million yacht explain why," *Business Insider*, July 16, 2018, https://www.businessinsider.com/how-putin-spends-his-mysterious-fortune-2017-6.

Principle #9

41. Seth Stephens-Davidowitz, "Don't Let Facebook Make You Miserable," *New York Times*, May 6, 2017, https://www.nytimes.com/2017/05/06/opinion/sunday/dont-let-facebook-make-you-miserable.html.

42. Phil Reed, Nazli I. Bircek, Lisa A. Osborne, Caterina Viganò, Roberto Truzoli. "Visual Social Media Use Moderates the Relationship between Initial Problematic Internet Use and Later Narcissism." *The Open Psychology Journal*, 2018; 11 (1): 163 DOI: 10.2174/1874350101811010163.

43. Mai-Ly Nguyen Steers, Robert E. Wickham and Linda K. Acitelli. "Seeing Everyone Else's Highlight Reels: How Facebook Usage Is Linked to Depressive Symptoms," October 2014 *Journal of Social and Clinical Psychology* 33(8): 701–731 DOI:10.1521/jscp.2014.33.8.701.

Principle #10

44. Robert A. Emmons and Michael E. McCullough, "Counting Blessings Versus Burdens: An Experimental Investigation of Gratitude and Subjective Well-Being in Daily Life," *Journal of Personality and Social Psychology*, American Psychological Association, Inc. 2003, Vol. 84, No. 2, 377–389. https://greatergood.berkeley.edu/pdfs/GratitudePDFs/6Emmons-BlessingsBurdens.pdf.

Principle #11

45. Tim Keller, Sermon: "Jesus' Prayer for All Time," Redeemer Presbyterian Church, November 25, 2007, https://podcast.gospelinlife.com/e/jesus-prayer-for-all-time/.

46. William J. Cromie, "Prayers don't help heart surgery patients," *Harvard Gazette*, April 6, 2006, https://news.harvard.edu/gazette/story/2006/04/prayers-dont-help-heart-surgery-patients-2/.

47. Press Release from Harvard Flourishing Program at Harvard's Institute for Quantitative Social Science, "Associations with Religious Upbringing," September 13, 2018, https://hfh.fas.harvard.edu/religious-upbringing.

48. Podcast Interview with Valerie Woerner (founder of Val Marie Paper), *Mere Christians Podcast*, February 23, 2022, https://podcast.jordanraynor.com/episodes/valerie-woerner-owner-of-val-marie-paper.

49. Randy Pope, Sermon: "Ready, Aim, Pray," February 17, 2013–March 24, 2013, Perimeter Church https://www.perimeter.org/messages/series/ready-aim-pray.

Principle #12

50. Jade Scipioni, "IT Cosmetics Jamie Kern Lima: 'I lived completely burnt out for almost a decade,'" March 9, 2021, CNBC, https://www.cnbc.com/2021/03/09/it-cosmetics-jamie-kern-lima-on-building-a-billion-dollar-company.html.

51. Michael Hyatt, "A Question That Changes Everything," Full Focus https://fullfocus.co/a-question-that-changes-everything/.

52. Mark Batterson and Jordan Raynor, "How to Live a Deep Life at Work and at Home," *Redeem the Day Podcast*, November 30, 2021, https://redeemthedaypodcast.com/episodes/how-to-live-a-deep-life-at-work-and-at-home/transcript.

53. Tim Keller, Sermon: "Your Plans: God's Plans," Redeemer Presbyterian Church, December 12, 2004, https://podcast.gospelinlife.com/e/jesus-prayer-for-all-time/. https://www.youtube.com/watch?v=3OXaJPiov5E.

54. Michael Hyatt, "A Question That Changes Everything," Full Focus https://fullfocus.co/a-question-that-changes-everything/.

Help Spread the Message of Reframing Career Success

Would you consider sharing this book with your networks on social media? It only takes a few minutes. For self-published authors, these efforts play a very important role in making the book visible to others. If posting on your social media channels, here are some suggestions:

- Highlight a quote that resonated with you.
- Note a key takeaway.
- Share your career success definition.
- Include the hashtag #ReframingCareerSuccess in your posts.

I also encourage you to leave an honest review of the book on Amazon. To do so:

1. Google "Reframing Career Success, Amazon."
2. Click on the "stars/rating" link that appears just under the title.
3. Click "Write a Customer Review" (at the time of this writing, this link appears on the left side towards the top of the page).

THANK YOU!!!

Additional Resources

1-to-1 Coaching

Thoughtful outside perspectives can go a long way to providing new direction, motivation and contentment. Connect with me for a 1-to-1 hour-long confidential coaching call that will focus on WHATEVER YOU WANT related to how the gospel message can be applied to the career challenges and successes you are grappling with today. This can include concerns like:

- Frustration that you never secured a certain job promotion;
- Disappointment that a particular entrepreneurial idea or creative idea has never caught on;
- The feeling that career aspirations have been derailed due to various circumstances beyond your control (i.e., an abusive narcissistic boss, unfair politics, personal tragedies, etc.);
- Stagnation and disenchantment with work; or
- Dissatisfaction even though you have achieved your big goals.

Based on your challenges, we'll talk about how you might act on some of the principles in this book.

Workshops

How can individuals and teams do their best work? Leaders and organizations spend considerable amounts of time and resources addressing this question. Often overlooked is the critical component of connecting faith to one's work. Workshops, conducted both virtually and in person, help teams and organizations consider how the gospel message can provide everlasting peace through the highs and lows of our career journeys.

I offer customized workshops based on the content in this book, leveraging my years of experience leading communications training sessions for different universities and brands. Through practical and interactive sessions, attendees will gain new perspectives about how the gospel message connects to one's work. This has the power to provide peace, contentment and motivation. Workshops are ideal for churches, universities, faith-based companies and non-profits, corporate chaplaincy programs and organizations' Christian employee network groups.

Purchase the Dry Erase "Career Success Definition and Metrics" Acrylic Photo Frame

You can purchase our 8x10 inch magnetic double-sided acrylic photo frame. On one side are the words "Career Success Definition." Flip it around, and you will see the words "Career Success Metrics." Both images feature lines for you to write out—and erase—your responses directly on the acrylic frame using a dry erase marker. When finished, keep this frame on your desk or place of work to remind yourself regularly about your career success definition and metrics! You can always update your responses. It is a little bit like a journal, except it is much more visible!

Learn more about these opportunities at
www.reframingcareersuccess.com.

About the Author

Kevin Anselmo is probably just like you! He has achieved some goals throughout his career and failed frequently. Professional setbacks have left him feeling down and out. He has been hard on himself when ideas haven't caught on. He has frequently questioned his own abilities and lost perspective in the face of career trials.

In response, Kevin has spent significant time considering and researching what success at work entails from a Christian perspective. This has provided him a sense of peace and motivation in how he works.

An ambitious entrepreneur, Kevin has been running his own communications consulting company—Experiential Communications—since 2013. He also started Global Innovators Academy, an experiential learning platform in which students and young professionals engage with entrepreneurs and innovators and then create content online based on their conversations. In conjunction with this book, Kevin offers coaching and workshops that focus on Christian principles for dealing with career ups and downs. Learn more at www.reframingcareersuccess.com.

Kevin resides in Sarasota, Florida, with his wife and two sons. He loves coaching his kids' youth basketball teams and is a member of South Shore Community Church.

www.ingramcontent.com/pod-product-compliance
Lightning Source LLC
Chambersburg PA
CBHW030305130626
46549CB00002B/699